"*Hope Beyond Our Sorrows* is the compassionate companion we all need while navigating life after loss. April Yamasaki's reflections are honest, acknowledging the pain of grief rather than trying to explain it away. Her advice is helpful, offering gentle ways to process different aspects of sorrow. And her posture is still full of hope, reminding us that in Christ, 'grief and broken dreams are not the end of the story.' The tender kindness she exudes through her writing makes this book a must-read for those grappling with different types of loss, as well as those who want to better support those who mourn."

KENDRA BROEKHUIS, author of the novels *Between You and Us* and *Nearly Beloved*

"Weaving together biblical stories like those of Elijah and Ruth with her own disorienting days and nights after the loss of her husband, April Yamasaki is a comforting arm around the shoulders to those walking through grief. Like Saint Brendan the Voyager as he set sail for the ancient Scottish Isles to see where God would lead him, Yamasaki tells us that grief is a peregrination, a journey where the destination is unknown. But hope is always seeking a home."

CHRISTIANA N. PETERSON, author of *Mystics and Misfits: Meeting God through St. Francis and Other Unlikely Saints* and *Awakened by Death: Life-Giving Lessons from the Mystics*

"I have never read a more timely book. April Yamasaki addresses both the pain and the hope of loss, something that most of us are deeply familiar with. When our hearts are broken by illness, death, or as it is for me, my husband's dementia, it is often hard to find hope and faith that draws us beyond our sorrows. Yamasaki's book is full of deep sadness, joy, and wisdom, with many practical suggestions on how to cope in the midst of sorrow. From the simple 'Get up and eat' to the need for courage and lament but also wonder and hope, *Hope Beyond Our Sorrows* has much to offer for anyone who is grieving a recent loss, be it of a spouse, a family member, or even a job—and this is probably all of us."

CHRISTINE SINE, author of multiple books, including *Digging Deeper: The Art of Contemplative Gardening* and *The Gift of Wonder: Creative Practices For Delighting in God*

"I have learned that the only way through grief is through. April Yamasaki lays out a unique, hopeful path to healing and wholeness in the now and not yet."

DORINA LAZO GILMORE-YOUNG, author of multiple books, including *Redeemer: God's Lovingkindness in the Book of Ruth* and *Breathing Through Grief: A Devotional Journal for Seasons of Loss*, from the foreword

Hope Beyond Our Sorrows

APRIL YAMASAKI

Foreword by Dorina Lazo Gilmore-Young

HOPE BEYOND OUR SORROWS

LEARNING TO LIVE WITH LIFE-CHANGING LOSS

Harrisonburg, Virginia

Herald Press
PO Box 866, Harrisonburg, Virginia 22803
www.HeraldPress.com

Library of Congress Cataloging-in-Publication Data applied for.

Study guides are available for many Herald Press titles at www.HeraldPress.com.

HOPE BEYOND OUR SORROWS
© 2025 by April Yamasaki. Released by Herald Press, Harrisonburg, Virginia 22803.
800-245-7894. All rights reserved.
Library of Congress Control Number: 2025006405
International Standard Book Number: 978-1-5138-1624-1 (paperback);
   978-1-5138-1625-8 (hardcover); 978-1-5138-1626-5 (ebook)
Printed in United States of America
Cover: Boomanoid / iStock / Getty Images Plus; vectortatu / iStock / Getty Images Plus;
Aleksey Selyanin / iStock / Getty Images Plus; zenstock / iStock / Getty Images Plus

All rights reserved. This publication may not be reproduced, stored in a retrieval system,
or transmitted in whole or in part, in any form, by any means, electronic, mechanical,
photocopying, recording or otherwise without prior permission of the copyright owners.
AI training is not permitted without specific licensing.

Unless otherwise noted, Scripture text is taken from the COMMON ENGLISH BIBLE. Copy-
right © 2011 COMMON ENGLISH BIBLE. All rights reserved. Used by permission.
   Scripture quotations marked (KJV) are taken from the King James Version.
   Scripture quotations marked (NCV) are taken from the New Century Version®. Copy-
right © 2005 by Thomas Nelson. Used by permission. All rights reserved.
   Scripture quotations marked (NIV) are taken from the Holy Bible, New International
Version®, NIV®. Copyright © 1973, 1978, 1984, 2011 by Biblica, Inc.® Used by permission
of Zondervan. All rights reserved worldwide. www.zondervan.com The "NIV" and "New
International Version" are trademarks registered in the United States Patent and Trademark
Office by Biblica, Inc.®
   Scripture quotations marked (NLT) are taken from the *Holy Bible, New Living Trans-
lation*, copyright © 1996, 2004, 2015 by Tyndale House Foundation. Used by permission of
Tyndale House Publishers, Inc., Carol Stream, Illinois 60188. All rights reserved.

29 28 27 26 25   10 9 8 7 6 5 4 3 2 1

For My Dearheart

CONTENTS

Foreword *11*
Introduction: How Can We Go On?. *13*

PART ONE: EARLY GRIEF
A Broken Heart

1. Breath *19*
2. Tears *25*
3. Food *31*
4. Rest *37*
5. Presence *43*
6. Silence *49*
7. Questions *55*
8. Guilt *61*
9. Anger *67*
10. Mourning *73*

PART TWO: MIDDLE GRIEF
A Hard Path

11. While It Was Still Dark *81*
12. The Journey of Grief *87*
13. The Losses We Carry *93*
14. When One Step Feels Like Too Much *99*
15. A Place to Start *105*
16. One Foot in Front of the Other *113*
17. Wisdom Along the Way *119*
18. The Courage to Keep Going *127*
19. From Me to We *133*
20. Sorrowful, Yet Rejoicing *139*

PART THREE: PRESENT GRIEF
A Way Forward

21. Remember the Wonders........................ 147
22. A Lovely Remembrance....................... 155
23. Every Life Leaves a Legacy 161
24. On Not Getting Over Grief.................... 167
25. Through Grief to Giving 175
26. A Changing Landscape 181
27. More Complicated Grief 189
28. No More Death, No More Grieving............. 195
29. God Restores All Things 203
30. God Comes to Us............................ 209

Afterword.................................... 215
Acknowledgments 217
Notes.. 219
The Author.................................. 223

FOREWORD

When I was widowed at age thirty-seven, I stepped onto a long, windy path of grief. I also found myself leading my three young daughters, ages two, five, and eight. I couldn't carry them. They had to find their own steps through grief, but I knew I had to courageously walk ahead and lead even though I had no idea where I was going. We embarked on a wildly disorienting journey.

My husband was diagnosed with stage four cancer in May of that year and soared to heaven in September. At the time, we were leading a flourishing nonprofit ministry together. Our kids were thriving. My husband had just turned forty and had grand plans for the year, including travel and triathlons, as well as chasing new dreams. All of that came to a screeching halt.

After his initial diagnosis, I experienced anticipatory grief because I did not know what our future held and dared not believe the worst. As a mother, I watched my children suffer as I was powerless to help them. After my husband died, the path of grief felt like a labyrinth—sometimes gently undulating forward, other times feeling like a trap with no exit. Despite being surrounded by community, I felt an indescribable ache and loneliness.

Hope Beyond Our Sorrows

Gratefully, God met me on that path. Just as he met Ruth on the road to Bethlehem, David in the cave where he hid, and Elijah when he was completely depleted, God met me. And that has made all the difference in my life.

In *Hope Beyond Our Sorrows*, April Yamasaki offers us a hand so we do not have to traverse the path of grief alone. She helps orient us while recognizing that each journey on the road of grief is unique and different. Through her tender stories, we are invited to reflect on our own experiences of loss and to acknowledge the pain. She gently guides us back to Scripture and tending to our grief in all of its facets. She gives us permission to cry, rage, ask questions, breathe, and remember.

April is a trusted voice. Not only does her story resonate as someone who has been widowed, but she has also served as a pastor and spiritual mentor for twenty-five years, offering words of comfort and hope to many who have endured different kinds of loss.

What I appreciate most about this book is that April leads us to lament. Grief is the sorrow we experience in loss, but lament is taking that sorrow to the feet of Jesus. Through the "hope practices" in this book, we are invited to enter into grief and, like the psalmists, continue to lay down our burdens in that grief. I have learned that the only way through grief is through. April lays out a unique, hopeful path to healing and wholeness in the now and not yet.

—Dorina Lazo Gilmore-Young
Author of multiple books, including
*Redeemer: God's Lovingkindness in the
Book of Ruth* and *Breathing Through Grief:
A Devotional Journal for Seasons of Loss*

INTRODUCTION

How Can We Go On?

Thirteen months after my Dearheart's death, I had a sudden impression: maybe I was ready to think about writing another book. My Dearheart—my Gary—had always been enthusiastic about my ministry both as a pastor and a writer. With his encouragement, I had published several books over the years. But since his death, I had written only short pieces—blog posts, sermons, teaching sessions, things that could be contained and completed in short bursts. In my early grief, I could hardly read a whole book, let alone think about writing one.

Most days I still felt too restless and overwhelmed by life to concentrate. So another book? I was surprised at the sudden flicker of thought. It was such a passing thought that when a writer friend asked, "Are you thinking about another book?" I had honestly said no. At most I was thinking about thinking about another book.

But then I received an email from a new editor at Herald Press. She congratulated me on the tenth anniversary of my first Herald Press book, *Sacred Pauses*, then asked if I might be interested in another book project. She even suggested a few ideas based on what she knew of my writing and speaking. Perhaps a book on burnout, since she had heard me speak on that subject. Or something related to my grief journey, since she had read some of my blog posts.

Her email gave me a lot to think about. Both burnout and the death of a spouse are life-changing losses. Both are about grief and healing, and I wondered whether I might be able to write a book focused on that part of the journey, on how we live through and with life-changing loss. Suddenly my passing thought about writing another book was more than simply passing through!

"But isn't it too early?" another friend asked. One of her other friends had written a book on grief, but that was twelve years after the death of her husband.

I suppose it was too early, for it was almost seven months before I submitted a formal book proposal, and another seven months before I could write and send a sample chapter. Even now, I wonder, how can I possibly write this book?

Some days I'm very much in the present—picking fresh rhubarb from my garden, hosting friends for lunch, planning a trip to visit family members at a distance, meeting another book review deadline, editing an article, preaching for my church, teaching a class, or doing any of a hundred other happy and productive things. But some days I'm back in my early grief, overwhelmed by mourning, too agitated to read, not wanting to do anything but feel sorry for myself, lie on the couch, and watch a classic DVD from my Dearheart's collection.

Introduction

I'm obviously not done with grieving, whatever "done with" might look like. And I know I'm not alone in this. I know many other women and men who grieve the loss of their life partner. Parents who have lived through the wrenching death of their child. Children and adults who have endured the deaths of parents and beloved grandparents. Those who have lost other family members and close friends and mentors. Those who have experienced the loss of health. The loss of a job. The loss of a home. The loss of a marriage. The loss of a church community. The loss of a cherished dream.

In the face of such devastating and life-changing loss, how can we go on? Can we go on?

I don't claim to have all the answers. Some days I don't think I have any answers at all. I know that for too many, grief is unbearable. Life is unbearable, and they sink under the weight of it. I'm at a loss for what to do or say or write that might make a difference. Yet I pray God's comfort for all who are weary and weighed down by grief. I pray God's rest for body, mind, soul, and spirit. I pray God's goodness and mercy to raise up those who are struggling, encourage the downcast, and work healing and renewal for all.

With this book, I bear witness to the faith and hope beyond our sorrows—in my own life and in the lives of people I know, in the wisdom of Scripture and in books I've read, from my experience in the church and in the world at large, and as one well acquainted with life's delayed, disappointing, and broken dreams. I bear witness that God's goodness and mercy are

Hope Beyond Our Sorrows

big enough for my soul's lament, big enough for your soul's lament too—longer and deeper and wider than our laments can ever be.

So may we be comforted and hold on to faith and hope beyond our sorrows. And when holding on seems impossible, may we know that God holds on to us. When a broken dream breaks our hearts, may we recover the lost art of dreaming, and learn to dream again. Even as we journey with grief, may we find a way forward, and live with faith and hope beyond our broken dreams. "May you have more and more mercy, peace, and love" (Jude 1:2).

—April Yamasaki

PART ONE

Early Grief
A Broken Heart

1

BREATH

Grief is not letting go. It is letting in. Grief is not moving on. It is moving with.

J. S. PARK, *As Long As You Need*

When my Dearheart and I married, we were both twenty-one and full of dreams. He was about to start law school. I was entering my fourth year of university, doing office work for a temp agency, and rediscovering my childhood dream of writing. We looked forward to a long and happy life together—loving God, loving each other, loving the work we felt called to do. The traditional wedding vows might be "till death do us part," but privately we both imagined a long and happy life together, stretching into eternity.

I'm grateful that we had almost forty-five years of married life—living our dreams, lamenting the broken ones, and learning to dream again. But we had both wanted more time together. We thought we had more time together. My Dearheart had come through cancer once before, and we prayed— our whole church prayed—that he would come through again. Despite the complications. Despite his three-week hospital stay that interrupted his chemotherapy. After all, the worst seemed to be over, and his doctors talked about him getting

Hope Beyond Our Sorrows

stronger, finally coming home from the hospital, and finally resuming his treatments. "You've done it before. You can do it again," the hospitalist said to him.

But suddenly he took a terrible turn for the worse, overcome by yet one more complication that proved to be fatal. No, no, no—how could this be? Just when he seemed to be getting better, my Dearheart was suddenly gone.

These days I sometimes still say, "No, no, no. It can't be!" I don't want to be without my Dearheart, without him by my side dreaming along with me. Some might say that I should be done with grieving by now, that it's time to move on. But even on my best days, grief is the air I breathe and the undercurrent of everything. And something in me doesn't want that to end. I want to go on grieving. As I'm learning, there is no moving on. There's only moving with.

Yet even as I journey with grief, I'm learning to dream again. Though our years together came to an abrupt end, I'm grateful for my Dearheart and the life we had together. Though the dreams we had for our lives were cut short, I hold onto faith and hope beyond my sorrows. And wonder of wonders, by God's goodness and mercy, I'm finding a way forward.

In my early grief, I couldn't read more than a few paragraphs at a time, so all the chapters in this book are divided into short sections. The first chapters are shorter than the rest and

Breath

bear a single-word title, and I've grouped all of the chapters in three parts:

- Part 1 Early Grief – A Broken Heart
- Part 2 Middle Grief – A Hard Path
- Part 3 Present Grief – A Way Forward

These three parts represent the three broad movements of my grief journey—not formal stages born of psychology or years of research, but my own lived experience. Some say that grief is like molasses, and I've found that analogy helpful. My early grief was like a sudden plunge into molasses where I felt stuck. I could hardly move or breathe. Middle grief was the struggle to get unstuck, to start dealing with the many tasks and the many "firsts" that follow a death or other life-changing loss. Present grief is the ongoing journey—the way forward more or less unstuck, but still with grief clinging like molasses.

These three movements unfold in this book with the chapters arranged accordingly, but you don't have to read them in any particular order. You might take a glance through the list of contents, and turn to the chapters that speak to you first. Or you might open the book at random and start reading, which I often do when I start a book. Just as we experience different losses throughout our lives, just as we grieve in different ways, we can read a book in different ways too. Feel free to read in whatever way seems most helpful or appealing or manageable to you, in order from beginning to end or in random segments.

At the end of each short chapter, I offer a practice or prayer that I or others have found helpful in our grieving. This is not

Hope Beyond Our Sorrows

more grief work to add to your to-do list. Not homework that must be done before turning the page. Instead, think of these as exercises in hope, as experiments that you might want to try, as examples that you might vary as you choose, as optional extras that you can come back to later or set aside completely if they don't seem a good fit. You have freedom to grieve in your own way.

Breath

HOPE PRACTICE

The loss of my Dearheart was enormous, so enormous that at times I could hardly breathe. So I practiced—practiced breathing to calm myself, practiced breathing to collect my thoughts. I would breathe in, breathe out. Breathe in God's presence. Breathe out anxiety and fear. Breathe in slowly, counting one, two, three, four, five. Breathe out even more slowly with a longer exhale, counting one, two, three, four, five, six, seven.

I had learned this calming rhythm when I was part of the book launch team for *Try Softer*, by trauma-informed counselor Aundi Kolber. From her book, I learned that the vagus nerve is the longest nerve in our bodies, connecting our brain with our heart, lungs, and digestive system. The vagus nerve reacts without our thinking about it, without our conscious choice, so when we feel threatened or anxious, we may find our heart racing, our breathing erratic, our digestive system upset. But research has shown that breathing with a longer exhale tells the vagus nerve that there is no danger, and helps to calm our heart rate, our breathing, our digestive system.[1]

Hope Beyond Our Sorrows

After reading *Try Softer*, I would practice breathing this way whenever I felt anxious. In my early grief, when I felt agitated, when I couldn't find the words to pray, breathing in this way became my prayer. Perhaps this prayer practice will be helpful to you as well.

Give yourself time and room to breathe.

Breathe in slowly: one, two, three, four, five. Breathe out even more slowly with a longer exhale: one, two, three, four, five, six, seven. Breathe in God's presence. Breathe out anxiety and fear. Repeat as often as necessary.

2

TEARS

If only my head were a spring of water, and my eyes a fountain of tears.

JEREMIAH 9:1

After my Dearheart died, I thought I might be consumed by the fountain of tears that Jeremiah longed for, that I might be consumed and totally undone by grief. Jeremiah, the weeping prophet, was so undone by his grief over the city of Jerusalem that he wrote the book of Lamentations. The brief book is aptly named, for its five chapters are an extended lament over the devastating loss. The city had been badly burned. Many of the people had been captured or killed, and those who remained were in desperate need.

The book of Lamentations begins with lament:

Oh, no!
She sits alone, the city that was once full of people.
Once great among nations, she has become like a widow.
Once a queen over provinces, she has become a slave.
—Lamentations 1:1

Lamentations also ends with lament:

Why do you forget us continually;
    why do you abandon us for such a long time?

Hope Beyond Our Sorrows

> Return us, LORD, to yourself. Please let us return!
>   Give us new days, like those long ago—
> unless you have completely rejected us,
>   or have become too angry with us.
> —Lamentations 5:20–22

Yet even in the midst of such grief, in the midst of such devastating and life-changing loss, Lamentations offers a word of hope. Though the people were consumed by their grief and tears and desperate situation, they would not be consumed and totally undone forever. Their story was not yet over. These verses of reassurance stand at the center of the book, in the midst of the people's deep grief:

> Certainly the faithful love of the LORD hasn't ended;
>   certainly God's compassion isn't through!
> They are renewed every morning. Great is your faithfulness.
> —Lamentations 3:22–23

I was in high school when I first read these verses in the King James Version of the Bible, and find myself returning to them again and again:

> It is of the LORD's mercies that we are not consumed,
>   because his compassions fail not.
> They are new every morning: great is thy faithfulness.
> —Lamentations 3:22–23 (KJV)

Our circumstances may not be as dire as the people of Lamentations, but for anyone grieving the loss of a loved one, the loss of a community, the loss of a dream—whatever

Tears

life-changing loss we might experience—our grief might threaten to consume us. We may become so overwhelmed by our grief that we can't focus on anything else. Our loss becomes our whole life.

For anyone dealing with health issues: the medical testing, the dreadful diagnosis, the expense and rigors of treatment, and the complicated medical system might threaten to undo us.

For those in the world of work: the financial realities, the pressures, the long hours, the politics can eat away at our time and energy and try our souls.

Those in school might be worn out by studying, exams, or peer pressure.

Families might be stressed to the breaking point by the fast pace of daily life, with too much to do, not enough time to do it, and more importantly, not enough time together. There is always something clamoring for our attention—another text, another email, another news flash, another something beeping at us.

Yet just as the burning bush that appeared before Moses was not consumed by its fire, we are not totally burned up or burned out by the things that might threaten to consume us. God is greater than those things. And just at the moment we might fear that God's compassion has failed us, Lamentations reminds us that God's compassions fail—not! God remains with us through whatever griefs we bear, whatever challenges we face.

To lament over loss is healthy and part of healing. We need to express our grief and sorrow. We need to honor our loss, with

Hope Beyond Our Sorrows

words and no words, with or without tears, or with wailing if need be. There's nothing wrong with a good cry. Tears can bring release and relief. Tears can be freeing. Researchers say that tears can be soothing, because they release feel-good hormones like oxytocin and endorphins. Weeping may endure for a night, but not forever.

Some find it helpful to set some limits around their tears. So if you'd rather not cry in public, then go to a room by yourself and shut the door. If you'd rather cry with someone instead of crying alone, then find that someone. After the death of her husband, one woman said she cried for a week, and then decided she was done with crying on her own; instead, she started a grief support group for herself and others.

As for me, I keep reminding myself that God's compassions fail—not! While I might be consumed by tears for a moment, it is of the Lord's mercies that I am not totally undone—not undone by tears or grief forever and all time, not undone by anything else in this life. Like Jeremiah, like the women wailing over the loss of their city, I can hope in God who is ever present and ever faithful, even in the midst of grief. The center still holds. In his commentary on Lamentations, professor and theologian Soong-Chan Rah confirms, "Hope is dependent on who God *is* rather than what we can do for ourselves."[1] So when hope seems elusive, when I am overcome by grief, still I wait on God. I hope in God who never fails.

Tears

HOPE PRACTICE

When you feel like crying, go ahead and have a good cry. Let yourself be consumed by your tears at least for a moment. Then as you recover, remember that God is faithful. It is of the Lord's mercies that you are not consumed forever and always.

In deep despair, the psalmist turns to God:

> You keep track of all my sorrows.
>> You have collected all my tears in your bottle.
>> You have recorded each one in your book.
>
> —Psalm 56:8 (NLT)

Imagine God collecting your tears. As signs of grief and love for whoever or whatever you've lost, your tears are precious. They matter, and God gathers them up.

3

FOOD

Grief is as natural as eating when you're hungry, drinking when you're thirsty, and sleeping when you're tired.
EARL A. GROLLMAN, "Grief Is Nature's Way of Healing a Broken Heart"

I had just started my second year of teaching at a local Bible college when my father died suddenly of a heart attack. It was the first death in my immediate family, and I hadn't realized that my grief would be so physical. Even when I wasn't consciously thinking of him or of his sudden passing, my body would react, and I would suddenly be on the verge of tears. When I saw what looked like his old Ford LTD driving down the street. Or when I saw an older Asian man looking over the produce at the grocery store as my father used to do. Dad would turn over an apple to look for bruises or pick up the bok choy to make sure it was fresh before he bought it. "They don't like to see me coming," he once said to me. I never did ask him whether he meant the storekeepers—or had he been joking about the produce?—but as far as I know the elusive "they" never protested. At any rate, he kept on carefully inspecting each item before he went to the checkout.

Years later, after my Dearheart's sudden death and before I left his bedside at the hospital, a social worker brought me a sandwich, some yogurt, and water. I appreciated her kindness and thanked her, but set everything aside. While grief may be as natural as eating when you're hungry, in times of grief, we may not feel hungry, and we may not feel like eating. My shock and grief were so physical that I couldn't eat. I couldn't even think about eating. Instead, I took the social worker's offering home, and it wasn't until the next day that I ate the sandwich, drank the water, and since I'm not a yogurt fan, I put the little cup in the freezer. "I'll make muffins with it later," I said to myself. And weeks later, I did.

My Dearheart's younger brother and his wife live about an hour and a half drive away from me. After my Dearheart's death, they started ordering food from restaurants in my area and having it delivered to me at home. They would text and ask, "Are you home tonight? We thought we would send you some food." The first time was a nice surprise and such a gift of care. But after the second, third, and fourth times, I wondered what was going on. "You need to eat," they said. A friend of theirs had lost her husband the previous year, and in her grief, she couldn't eat and had lost a dangerous amount of weight. "We just want to make sure you're eating."

Others came with soup, bread, dumplings, homemade brownies, cookies, a selection of specialty teas and other beverages. "Is your freezer still full of lasagna?" someone asked me months later, and yes, I still had lasagna waiting for me. My freezer was full of food and kindness.

Food

Elijah was fiercely loyal to the Lord God, and fiercely critical of King Ahab and Queen Jezebel for following other false gods. When they threatened to kill him, he ran away as far and as fast as he could. He ran until he could run no more. Then, alone in the wilderness, Elijah fell exhausted under a lonely tree.

In fear, grief, and desperation, Elijah prayed for God to take his life. He would rather have God end his life in the wilderness instead of falling into the hands of the royal couple.

But instead of ending Elijah's life, God provided for his needs. Elijah fell into a deep sleep, until an angel woke him and said, "Get up and eat" (1 Kings 19:5 NIV). There beside him was a loaf of bread and a jug of water, so Elijah ate and drank, then fell back asleep. Again an angel woke him and said, "Get up and eat, for the journey is too much for you" (1 Kings 19:7 NIV).

We might say that Elijah had a severe case of burnout. The journey *was* too much for him. His conflict with Ahab and Jezebel had been long and extremely stressful. He had lost his sense of safety. He had lost his sense of mission and purpose. He was exhausted in body, soul, and spirit. He had no more fight left in him, and he was too bone weary to continue his flight. He could hardly think straight. He could hardly stay awake. And God began to minister to him by first addressing his physical needs with food, water, and rest. Elijah was "refreshed by that food" (1 Kings 19:8) and continued his journey.

Food

HOPE PRACTICE

In periods of ministry burnout, in the loss of a loved one, in other experiences of life-changing loss, the journey may also be too much for us. Like Elijah, we may be exhausted in body, soul, and spirit. We may feel bone weary, yet have trouble sleeping. Or we may feel like sleeping night and day, yet never feel completely rested. We may not want to eat. We may not feel thirsty. We may find ourselves unable to finish daily tasks or even to notice what needs doing. We may feel confused and unable to make decisions. We may have difficulty praying.

When the journey is too much for us, when we're overwhelmed by the many challenges we face and unable to meet them, instead of trying in vain to address them all at once, perhaps we might start as the angel directed Elijah: get up and eat.

When my Dearheart was in the hospital, I didn't always eat right or at the right times, so I tried to have ready-to-eat food available: granola bars, fruit, nuts. A friend of a friend was so kind to send me some of her smoked salmon, along with a rice mix and a can of corn, because she didn't want me to have to think about what to make for supper. Even now I like to have

Food

some ready-made food in the freezer for those days when life and grief seem to press in on me: my homemade split pea soup, chili, and daikon pancakes, plus special treats like chocolate and ice cream.

In grief, and at other times of stress, some may turn to food for comfort. Plain potato chips have long been my favorite comfort food. My father had been in the snack food business, and my sisters and I often refer to potato chips as a family staple or even as a "condiment" that goes before, after, or with any meal. But a little comfort food can go a long way, so I try to measure out a portion of potato chips so I don't end up eating the whole family-size bag!

If you haven't yet had anything to eat or drink today, or if you haven't had anything in the last few hours, drink some water and eat something that tastes good and is good for you. That may depend on your particular food preferences, health requirements, and dietary restrictions including any allergies. But like Elijah, get up and eat, have a drink of water, and allow God's gifts of healthy food and clean water to strengthen you for the journey.

If your grief is causing you to lose weight or to overindulge in comfort food in a way that's unhealthy, if like Elijah you feel so desperate that you would rather God end your life, please call a crisis line; speak to a family member or friend; consult a pastor, doctor, counselor, or other health practitioner. Self-care practices like eating and drinking are essential, but they are not the only avenues of God's grace and care for us. Other physical, mental, and spiritual health supports are available. If reaching out seems overwhelming, start with just one call.

4

REST

Rest is not an optional extra of grief.

SYLVIA PURDIE, *Moving On: Grief in Ministry Transitions*

My Dearheart used to say that sleeping was my superpower. While he might wake up several times during the night, I would generally fall asleep and wake up refreshed seven or eight hours later. I would often still be in the same position as if I hadn't moved all night.

But the night my Dearheart died, I hardly slept. When I got home, I couldn't help but think back to one of my mother's best friends: my Aunty Margaret, who passed away years ago, and whose husband and son were lost at sea years earlier. I was still in high school, but I remember my mother telling me that when Aunty Margaret received word that her husband and son were lost, she turned on all the lights in the house and left them on until morning. Perhaps the light gave her comfort on that dark night. Perhaps it expressed her longing and waiting for her husband and son to come home, although they never did.

That night when I came home from the hospital alone, I too turned on all the lights on the main floor of our house and left them on until morning. After driving home in the dark, I couldn't bear for the house to be dark too. I felt cold, and couldn't warm up. I was exhausted, yet too restless to sleep. I knew my Dearheart wasn't coming home as we had hoped and prayed and expected. I wasn't waiting for him, yet still I left the lights on.

Perhaps I was keeping watch in a different way. Longing for consolation in the midst of deep grief. Longing for calm in the midst of the overwhelming cascade of emotions. Longing for light to lead me in this new wilderness.

When Elijah ran into the wilderness, he ran so hard and became so exhausted that when he finally stopped running, he fell into a deep sleep. He woke up only when an angel touched him on the shoulder, woke up only long enough to eat some of the freshly baked bread that had been prepared for him and to drink some water. Then, again, Elijah fell into a deep sleep. Again the angel woke him, he ate more bread and drank more water, and only then continued on his journey.

For Elijah, rest was essential. Rest and recovery for his aching muscles. Rest from the agonizing thought that he would be better off if God would end his life. Rest from the worry, fear, and grief that had sent him into the wilderness. Only after some time of rest was Elijah able to go on with his journey.

In *Moving On: Grief in Ministry Transitions*, author and editor Sylvia Purdie highlights rest as a key starting point in working through grief. She writes, "The brain and the body must have space to uncurl. The soul must breathe if it is to heal."[1] For Elijah and for us today, for anyone grieving a ministry transition, or grieving any kind of loss, rest gives us room to uncurl and heal.

Rest

When our sleep is disturbed by grief, or stress, or too much screen time, or due to any other reason, we may be more vulnerable to colds, flus, and other illnesses. Long-term lack of sleep has been associated with obesity, diabetes, and cardiovascular disease. We may not think as clearly or quickly as usual. We may have trouble remembering things. We may feel more irritable. We may fall asleep at odd times when we want to be awake.

According to sleep researchers, a good night's sleep helps our bodies recover from the rigors of the day, boosts our immune system, and promotes healing. Our minds process the day's events, discarding unnecessary information, and forming the rest into memories. At the deeper levels of sleep, our bodies and minds rest, so we wake refreshed and able to think clearly. We dream, perhaps as a way of sorting out our thoughts and feelings from the day that was, or rehearsing for the day to come.

Rest

HOPE PRACTICE

If grief disturbs your night-time sleep, know that you have lots of company. At one point, the psalmist too experienced such grief that he couldn't sleep:

> I'm worn out from groaning.
>> Every night, I drench my bed with tears;
>> I soak my couch all the way through.
>
> My vision fails because of my grief;
>> it's weak because of all my distress.
>
> —Psalm 6:6–7

If you're on the verge of becoming seriously sleep deprived, talk to your doctor or other health practitioner. Otherwise, just be gentle with yourself. Sleep when you can, but don't force it or scold yourself when you can't. Instead, you might try resting even if you're not able to fall asleep. Lie down, or sit and put your feet up. Close your eyes, unclench your muscles, and let your body sink into your bed or chair. Breathe. Make this your spiritual practice: to receive God's gift of rest.

Rest

If you find yourself nodding off, let yourself be carried into sleep. As the psalmist writes at another time:

I will lie down and fall asleep in peace
>   because you alone, LORD, let me live in safety.
—Psalm 4:8

If you don't fall asleep, may this part of the verse still hold true for you as you rest: "I will lie down . . . because you alone, LORD, let me live in safety."

5

PRESENCE

One of the contradictions in grief . . . is the need for solitude versus social support. Which is better? The answer is both.

ALAN WOLFELT, "Solitude or Social Support in Grief? Why We Need Both"

As I drove home from the hospital in the midwinter dark and rain, I thought to myself, "The world is weeping." A steady shower of tears from the sky now that my Dearheart was gone from me. My windshield wipers slapping away in vain, as the tears kept coming. The trees at the side of the road shedding rain and sorrow, washing all our hopes and dreams away.

Then finally home at my front door, I saw a splash of yellow. Daffodils! In a vase and with a card. But how would anyone know to bring me flowers? Who would leave a card? Apart from the staff, I had been alone at the hospital with my Dearheart. The end had come so quickly that I hadn't called anyone.

On the front of the card, a pair of golden-crowned kinglets perched on pine branches—oh, my Dearheart and me, I thought, only one of us is gone now. Inside I read:

Dear April,
   Just a little pick-me-up after a busy week. We are thinking of you!
   Love, Malonie and Helene

I knew my two friends had planned to spend the afternoon together, and they had known I would be at the hospital. Yet they had remembered me with daffodils, arranged them in a vase, chosen a lovely card, written a note, and delivered everything to my door. What a bright reminder of the presence of friends on that dark and lonely night!

Suddenly I realized I wasn't so alone.

Once Elijah had rested in the wilderness, once he had eaten some bread and drunk some water, he continued his journey until he came to Mount Horeb. There God had met Moses, given the people the ten commandments, and there, God met Elijah. God addressed him personally, "Why are you here, Elijah?" (1 Kings 19:9).

Elijah replied:

> I've been very passionate for the LORD God of heavenly forces because the Israelites have abandoned your covenant. They have torn down your altars, and they have murdered your prophets with the sword. I'm the only one left, and now they want to take my life too!
> —1 Kings 19:10

Yes, Elijah had been passionate for the Lord God. He had confronted King Ahab and Queen Jezebel for abandoning

Presence

God's covenant. Yes, they wanted to take his life, so he fled from them as fast and as far as he could. Yes, Elijah was alone in the wilderness.

Yet despite his litany of woe, it seems to me that Elijah wanted to be alone. After all, he had fled with his servant, but when they reached Beer-sheba—the southernmost city of Judah, on the edge of the desert—Elijah left his servant there. Perhaps he thought that his servant would be safe enough in Beer-sheba. Perhaps he thought he might travel faster and further alone. But the fact remains: Elijah could have brought his servant with him to Mount Horeb; instead, he chose to travel alone.

At the same time, Elijah was clearly disturbed at being alone. The other prophets had been murdered. The rest of the people had abandoned God's covenant. I can almost hear Elijah wailing, "I am the only one left!"

When we feel burdened by grief, we might feel as alone as Elijah did in the wilderness. We might also wail, "I'm the only one left!" because we want and need the company of others. At the same time, we might also want to be alone. We might want to hold others at a distance, just like Elijah left his servant in Beer-sheba and went to Mount Horeb alone. I realize that seems contradictory and messy. Grief is full of contradictions and conflicting feelings.

When my Dearheart was suddenly gone, I felt so alone that just the sight of daffodils at my door made me feel less lonely. I needed that reminder of the presence of people in my life. But when my sisters immediately asked if they should come stay

Hope Beyond Our Sorrows

with me, I said no. COVID-19 restrictions had started to ease, but there were still cautions about traveling and gathering in homes. Besides, for all their caring, I knew that the loneliness I felt couldn't be relieved by them or anyone. Even now, I often feel more lonely when I'm surrounded by others than when I'm home alone by myself. It's as if the presence of others magnifies the absence of my Dearheart.

Yet in my early grief, at times I wanted and needed to be with other people. I went for walks every day, most often with a family member or friend. I would spend hours on the phone. Some days I would talk with one or all three of my sisters, often in separate hour-long phone calls. Then I'd have another hour-long phone call with my Dearheart's older brother or with a friend. At other times, when the phone calls seemed too much, I'd let them go to voicemail and return them the next day or days later.

Sometimes I wanted to be alone, sometimes I craved conversation, and often I didn't know what I wanted. Grief made me a stranger to myself, and I'm grateful for those who let me be that way—without judging, without labeling me introvert or extrovert or ambivert, without cajoling me to be more one way or the other.

Presence

HOPE PRACTICE

Allow yourself to feel the way you feel: to be alone or with others, to want both at the same time or not know what you want. Such mixed feelings are not uncommon among those who grieve. A manager fired from his job says, "I miss going out for lunch with my co-workers, but I just can't face them." A woman grieving the death of her child says, "I really want to go to church to worship and be with other people, but it's just too hard."

If you'd rather be alone for a time, turn off your phone or let any calls go to voicemail. If someone invites you to supper, you can say thank you for the invitation, but you have other plans for that evening—even if your plan is simply to be at home alone. When a friend offered to come with me to the bank or to other appointments if I wanted company, I appreciated her kind offer. "But I think I need to do those things by myself," I said. "Let's go for coffee some other time."

If you'd like people to be more present in your life, don't be afraid to let them know. I will sometimes call one of my sisters. Or text a friend and ask, "I'm thinking about you—can we go for

Hope Beyond Our Sorrows

a walk?" Consider joining a grief support group or a Bible study, or signing up for a class online or in person.

If even thinking about these things makes you feel tired, don't feel pressured to act immediately. Instead, be gentle with yourself and your mix of thoughts and feelings. In grief, both solitude and social interaction have their place, and over time you will find the balance that's best for you.

For now, may you find comfort in the presence of God with these words from one of my favorite old hymns, written in 1847 by Henry Francis Lyte:

> Abide with me! fast falls the eventide.
> The darkness deepens; Lord, with me abide.
> When other helpers fail and comforts flee,
> Help of the helpless, O abide with me.
>
> Swift to its close ebbs out life's little day.
> Earth's joys grow dim, its glories pass away.
> Change and decay in all around I see.
> O thou who changest not, abide with me.
>
> I fear no foe, with thee at hand to bless.
> Ills have no weight, and tears no bitterness.
> Where is death's sting? where, grave, thy victory?
> I triumph still, if thou abide with me.[1]

6

SILENCE

Grief is the loudest silence I have ever heard.
ANGIE CARTWRIGHT, founder of National Grief Awareness Day

Elijah spent the night in a cave on Mount Horeb, and the next morning, God again spoke to him:

Go out and stand at the mountain before the LORD. The LORD is passing by.
—1 Kings 19:11

Elijah heard a strong wind sweeping down the mountain and breaking the rocks in its path. After the wind, he felt an earthquake. After the earthquake, he could see flames of fire outside the entrance to his cave. After the fire, he heard a sound: "Thin. Quiet" (1 Kings 19:12).

Then Elijah stood at the entrance of the cave, and heard again the word of the Lord: "Why are you here, Elijah?" (1 Kings 19:13). It was the same pointed question as before, and Elijah answered as he had before. While the people had been unfaithful, he had been passionate for the Lord God, so passionate that he was now under threat of death. "I'm the only one left," he said (1 Kings 19:14).

Then God answered Elijah with a new vision and a new mission. God directed him to go through the wilderness once

Hope Beyond Our Sorrows

more, this time past Beer-sheba in the south to the city of Damascus in the north. There he was to anoint Hazael to be king of Aram, Jehu to be king of Israel, and Elisha to be his successor. What's more, God had preserved seven thousand faithful followers. Elijah was wrong. He was not the only one left!

Perhaps it was grief that Elijah heard on the mountain: "Thin. Quiet" (1 Kings 19:14). Grief over those who had turned away from God's covenant. Grief over his own weariness from the fight with Ahab and Jezebel. Grief over his long flight for his life and the sense of being abandoned by everyone, or so it seemed.

But God had not abandoned him. God was with him in whatever storm he faced, no matter the size of the boulders crashing around him, no matter how much he was shaken, no matter the ordeals he faced. God would meet his needs. Just as God had provided Elijah with rest, food, and water on the first part of his journey, now God gave him a new purpose, and would lead him forward to discover other faithful followers and to mentor a new generation as he anointed Elisha to take his place.

In grief, there is a vast silence. When there's a death in the family, those who grieve often find that after the first few days of calls and caring, the phone no longer rings. People don't

Silence

stop by. The condolence cards stop coming. In the midst of grief, it may seem that God is silent too.

After the death of her husband, one woman said the house was too quiet, so she would try to go out every evening. Another always has the television or radio on during the day and watches YouTube videos on her phone at night until she falls asleep. On the death of her sister, another woman felt she had lost her sister and perhaps lost her faith too, for God seemed strangely silent.

On days when I've had too much silence, I turn on some music, call a family member or friend, or get out in my garden where neighbors often pass by and stop to chat.

At other times, the world seems too noisy to me. I can't take one more phone call from a real estate agent wanting to sell my townhouse or a political party wanting my vote. I'm bothered by the news—by stories of war and disasters, sexual assaults and horrible car accidents. I just want to turn everything off, and I do.

In silence, I find some relief. In silence, I find room to grieve and hear from God. I find comfort in the words of the prophet: "In return and rest you will be saved; quietness and trust will be your strength" (Isaiah 30:15). It was only in the silence that followed the storm and the earthquake and the fire that Elijah was able to hear God's new direction for his life. It was only in the silence that he realized he was not alone.

However deep and unexpected our grief might be, how overwhelming our circumstances, we are not alone. As God was

Hope Beyond Our Sorrows

with Elijah, God is with us too. When the house seems too quiet, God is with us. When the world seems too noisy, God is with us.

The book of Romans asks:

Who will separate us from Christ's love? Will we be separated by trouble, or distress, or harassment, or famine, or nakedness, or danger, or sword?
—Romans 8:35

In times of grief, when we might have trouble hearing the voice of God, when we might struggle to feel God's presence, we might well wonder: will we be separated from God's love by grief, or silence, or the death of our loved one, the death of a dream, or our own fragile faith? Can any of these things separate us from the love of Christ?

Romans clearly says, NO! Nothing can separate us from the love of Christ. Because of God's love, we can survive these things that might stand in our way and even overcome them: "in all these things we win a sweeping victory through the one who loved us" (Romans 8:37).

To make sure we get the point, Romans lists a number of specific things that will not separate us from the love of God: "not death or life, not angels or rulers, not present things or future things, not powers or height or depth, or any other thing that is created" (Romans 8:38–39).

The pairs of opposites in this list are meant to include everything in between: so death and life, and everything in between; things present and things to come, and everything in between; height and depth, and everything in between. If that weren't exhaustive enough, the list also includes angels, rulers,

Silence

powers, and any other created thing. There is no *who* or *what* that can separate us from the love of God.

The hardship of death is real, but it cannot separate us from the love of God. The pain of loss is real, but it cannot separate us from the love of God. The silence of grief is real, but it cannot separate us from the love of God.

Silence

HOPE PRACTICE

As I sit at home in silence, I begin to notice the small sounds around me. The tick of the second hand on my clock in the kitchen. The low hum of the fridge. My neighbor starting his truck. The coo of a mourning dove in the distance, or maybe it's an owl—I don't know my birds. The silence is not really silent, and I take comfort in these small sounds stirring. There are signs of life in this silence. God is in this silence.

Sit for a moment, and notice the sounds around you. What signs of life do you hear? If there's too much noise, what would you like to tone down? If it seems too quiet, you may wish to turn on some music. Then choose one of the following, and listen as God speaks to you in Scripture: Psalm 34:4; Isaiah 30:15; Matthew 11:28–30; Romans 8:38–39; Revelation 3:20.

7

QUESTIONS

My God! My God, why have you left me all alone?
PSALM 22:1

When my Dearheart was first diagnosed with cancer, he never asked, *Why me?* Unlike the psalmist who felt abandoned by God and raised hard questions, my Dearheart seemed to accept his diagnosis and the surgeon's recommendation. "This is just a blip," he said to me, and as it turned out, he was right. The surgery was successful, he recovered well, and we took a trip to Hawaii to celebrate.

Six years later when my Dearheart was diagnosed with the recurrence of cancer, and even when he faced complication after complication, he never asked, *Why me?*

Why not me? he would say. *Why not us?* From his study of the Bible and theology, and from what he had seen of life, he knew that bad things can happen at any time and to anyone. None of us are exempt from hardship and suffering in this world. From his Japanese heritage, he valued resilience in the face of adversity: when the wind rises, the bamboo sways and bends, but does not break. Its flexibility shows its strength and makes it more resilient than an oak tree. In the same way, when adversity comes, the one who moves with it is the one who overcomes.

After my Dearheart died, I rarely asked, *Why me? Why us?* Perhaps by then, I had so thoroughly adopted his perspective. Perhaps by then, I was well past asking. And all too soon, I was busy with other people's questions.

When will the funeral be?
When can we get together for coffee?
When will you come back to worship?
When will you be ready to speak in person?
When? When? When? When?

At times I had an answer. *Instead of gathering in person, there will be an online memorial.* COVID-19 pandemic protocols had started to ease, but many were still cautious about gathering and told me if there were a funeral, they would not attend. Others were following through on long-postponed travel plans and would be away. My Dearheart had willingly gone to funerals out of respect for others and to offer support, but I knew he didn't care to have one for himself. His brothers and other family members said, "Do whatever you and Gary would want."

At times I responded to questions with questions of my own. *Instead of coffee, could we go for a walk in the park? What time works for you?* Sometimes I put off answering. *I can't even think about that right now.* Or more simply, *I don't know.*

Even the most everyday questions were suddenly too hard for me. "How are you?" someone would ask. I couldn't say, because I didn't know myself. Most often I would respond with whatever I happened to be doing at the moment. *I'm just making tea*, I'd say to a friend on the telephone. *I'm on my way to pick up the mail*, I'd say to a neighbor. "You've been a pastor and walked with many grieving people," someone said to me, "but now that you're grieving yourself, what most surprises you?" At first, I could only stare at him, then finally replied, *Everything*.

Acquaintances that I hardly knew would sometimes ask what I thought were highly personal questions. What kind of cancer did he have? Did he pass peacefully? I would often think to myself, *Why are you asking? I don't know you well enough for this conversation*. But then the person would share his own struggle with cancer and tell me about his ongoing treatments. Or someone else would share about her father who was dying, and I understood her fear that his end might be more painful than peaceful. I realized that the questions people asked were often more about their own personal lives than mine. And sometimes well-meaning people would ask the most awkward questions because they didn't know what else to say. I could hardly take offense and tried to answer gently.

Are there better, less intrusive questions? Perhaps it is wiser not to ask any questions at all. One grieving woman comments, "The less you say is best. A hug and 'I love you' goes a long way." Textile artist Lois Klassen drew on her own experience to create a quilt of heart motifs on the theme of grief. One heart features various phrases like *Every cloud has a silver lining* and *Grin and bear it*. But the caption reads, "In the presence of a grieving heart, silence is kinder than words." The center of the heart motif expresses this more bluntly: *Shut up!* As another friend says, "The best thing you can do is listen. No one needs your opinion, just your support, love, and blessings."

Hope Beyond Our Sorrows

On the night my Dearheart passed away, I was scheduled to preach the next morning. Of course, when everyone at the church heard about his sudden passing, they understood why I wasn't there. That Sunday, the worship service went on without me, and the next, and the next. When would I come back to worship? I didn't know. When would I preach in person again? I didn't know.

I've been told many times, "You'll know when you're ready." When one pastor lost his wife to cancer, he took six months off before resuming his ministry at the church. Another pastor who was widowed took a year. Others take a few weeks or months. Some return to part-time ministry. Some retire or change churches. Perhaps they were also told, "You'll know when you're ready."

I wasn't sure that I'd know when I would be ready for the different responsibilities, invitations, and opportunities that awaited my answer. Or if I would ever feel ready for them.

When my Dearheart asked me to marry him when we were both eighteen years old and in our first year of university, was I ready then? Now when I look at eighteen-year-olds, I think I must have been too young. When I was called into pastoral ministry on an interim basis, when I received a continuing term as a lead pastor, when I was ordained—at each step along the way, I remember thinking, "Am I ready? This church seems more ready than I am for my new role and responsibilities."

I wasn't ready for my Dearheart to be diagnosed with cancer the first time, or the second time. I wasn't ready for his long hospital stay during the pandemic. I wasn't ready for him

Questions

to leave me so suddenly. His passing still seems sudden to me, and I'm still not ready to be without him.

Yet here I am. Ready or not. Despite the questions. Despite my lack of answers. That's true for so much of life. Things come to us unbidden. Life happens when we're busy doing other things and turns us around. Grief happens when we're busy doing other things and turns us around and around, even when we're not ready.

Questions

HOPE PRACTICE

Like the psalmist, perhaps you're wrestling with hard questions: Why me? Why now? Where are you, God? Even if you don't have the answers, you may find it helpful to record your questions, to set them down in writing and contain them on a page. Instead of letting them take over your day or disturb your sleep, commit them to God to keep your questions.

Perhaps you're weary of questions—the questions that you ask yourself, the questions that others may ask you, the questions that you can't—or don't want to—answer. Feel free to set them aside and not answer. It's all right to say I don't know. Or I can't talk about that. You don't have to answer every question just because it's asked.

The Serenity Prayer is often associated with addiction recovery: "God, grant me the serenity to accept the things I cannot change; the courage to change the things I can; and the wisdom to know the difference." When it comes to too many questions, I find this adaptation helpful and offer it to you as a prayer: God, grant me the serenity to wait on the questions I cannot answer; the courage to set aside those that don't need answering; and the wisdom to know the difference.

8

GUILT

When loss attacks, guilt is usually not far behind.
GARY ROE, *Comfort for Grieving Hearts*

In my early grief, the one question I kept asking myself was this: Why was I so consumed by grief, when others have lived through so much worse? Just a few days after my Dearheart died, Russia invaded Ukraine in a major expansion of their ongoing conflict. My country was not a war zone. I wasn't having to flee for safety. I wasn't grieving a loved one killed in battle. "You're not the only one who has lost a spouse," I would tell myself. Besides, we'd had a good life together, a good last day together, even though he was still in the hospital.

That day as we talked with his medical team about how he could get stronger to come home, my Dearheart said he was tired of hospital food. He'd like some wonton soup for lunch.

"Great idea," said his doctor.

"Wonderful," said his dietician.

So I got take-out from one of our favorite restaurants and brought him the wonton soup. I spooned some into a bowl I had brought from home, using one of our rice-patterned Chinese soup spoons. "You're so good to me," he said. He savored each wonton as we watched the Olympics together and as he explained the intricacies of curling to me.

But then he was overcome with one last complication. One moment he seemed fine, the next engulfed in pain. Still I was able to be at his side. Still I was able to say "I love you" one more time. Before he passed from this life to the next, his last words to me were, "I love you." Some might even call it a good death, for the end came quickly, we were together as he would have wanted, we had time to say goodbye, his favorite nurse was on shift, the emergency response team did what they could. But still he was gone. Still I felt devastated.

The Holmes and Rahe Stress Scale rates the death of a spouse as the most stressful life event with an impact score of 100. Divorce has an impact score of 73. The death of a close family member 63. Fired at work 47. House foreclosure 30. But the scale does not focus exclusively on loss, for it also includes more celebratory life events. Marriage is given an impact score of 50. Vacation 13. Christmas and other major holidays 12.

Psychiatrists Thomas Holmes and Richard Rahe developed this scale in the 1960s as part of their study on the relationship between stress and illness. They examined the medical records and life events of over five thousand patients and discovered a positive correlation. More stressful life events seemed to point to a greater likelihood of illness. Rahe did a follow-up study with twenty-five hundred US sailors. Other researchers have studied different ethnic and cultural groups in the United States and beyond. More recently, there have been attempts to update Holmes and Rahe's original scale.

Guilt

When I look at their list of life events, I can't help but wonder. Is the death of a spouse really the most stressful life event, more stressful than the death of a child? Does being fired at work have the same impact whether or not it was for cause, no matter how the firing was carried out or communicated? And what about those who experience multiple losses at the same time?

While there may be a place for psychiatrists and other specialists to quantify and compare for research purposes, loss is more complicated than a single rating scale or a single study. Loss is personal, with each person experiencing loss differently, and each loss having its own depth and particular details. On a personal level, the loss of my Dearheart had been devastating, but when I thought of others who had lost multiple family members under horrific circumstances, I felt guilty for my grieving, as if it were somehow wrong for me to grieve so deeply.

Jerry Sittser and his family were on their way home when a drunk driver drove into their car, killing Jerry's wife, their daughter, and his mother. Jerry and his three other children survived, but how horrible for them all, I thought. The loss of a spouse is hard, but surely the loss of three loved ones gone in an instant, the loss of three generations was much worse. Yet Sittser writes:

> Whose loss is worse? The question begs the point. What good is quantifying loss? What good is comparing? The right question to ask is not, "Whose is worse?" It is to ask,

Hope Beyond Our Sorrows

"What meaning can be gained from suffering, and how can we grow through suffering?"[1]

I appreciate the way Sittser shifts his focus even in the midst of grief. Although he had suffered terrible loss, he grew to look beyond it to the bigger picture of how he might learn and grow. Like him, I needed to shift my focus too. To stop feeling guilty, I didn't need to stop grieving. I needed to shift my focus to the bigger picture of meaning and growth.

After her mother's death, sixteen-year-old Anne Peterson felt guilty because she hadn't talked with her mother, who had called the night before she died. To make matters worse, her father said to her, "It's your fault your mother is dead." Years later, she would write, "I wore guilt like an ill-fitted jacket."[2] She was not responsible for her mother's death, and when she was finally able to tell her father how much his words had hurt her, he apologized for his accusation. He said that he was sorry that he hadn't been a good father to her. She could finally shed her ill-fitted jacket of false guilt and forgive him.

Others may feel guilty for making it through an accident when their companions died. Or they feel guilty over things said or left unsaid, things done or left undone—like the sister whose last conversation with her brother was one of anger, the adult son who was not at the hospital when his father died alone. As Gary Roe writes, "I could have. I should have. If only I hadn't. If only I had. I wish. What if. The guilt list has no end."[3] But whatever our guilt, real or imagined, there is a bigger picture of how we might grow and learn even in the midst of grief.

Guilt

HOPE PRACTICE

Sometimes I still feel guilty for grieving. And maybe you do too. Or maybe you blame yourself because you didn't say goodbye and I love you and all the things that you could have, or should have, or wanted to say. Maybe you said some things that you now regret and want to take back.

If you're feeling guilty for something you did or didn't do or say, you may find it helpful to write a letter to your loved one. Be honest about your feelings. Write down all of your If onlys and What ifs. But look at the bigger picture too of God's grace and forgiveness, of how you might grow and learn even in the midst of your grief.

If writing a letter feels like too much at this time, then set that idea aside. For now, it may be enough simply to sit with your grief and not compare it to anyone else's, to stop judging what you did or didn't do against some imagined ideal. Instead, release any guilty feelings by confessing those things you've done or left undone, and gratefully receive God's forgiveness and grace.

Sit comfortably in a chair with your hands face up in your lap. Feel the weight of whatever real or imagined guilt you carry,

Hope Beyond Our Sorrows

whatever regrets you may have stored up. Then raise your arms in front of you, stretch them out, and release that burden to God. Let God fill you instead with mercy and forgiveness. Receive the peace that passes all understanding. Then lower your arms, fold your hands in your lap, and give thanks for God's abundant grace.

9

ANGER

*Biblical lament is an act of protest, expressing grief,
anxiety, rage, and complaint against God.*
JONI S. SANCKEN, *All Our Griefs to Bear*

If anyone suffered as much as Job, it was Job's wife. Together the two had lost all of their livestock and all of their servants except for the few who survived to tell them the terrible news. Together they mourned the deaths of their sons and daughters, who had been killed when a desert storm caused the house they were in to collapse. Then Job was afflicted with sores all over his body, so severe that his pain and grief drove him out of the house to sit in a pile of ashes and scrape at his skin with a broken piece of pottery. Job's wife was left to bear her grief alone and to care for Job as best she could. Even their togetherness in suffering had been taken away from them.

Jewish legend says that the once wealthy woman became a water carrier to support Job and herself. But when her employer learned that she was Job's wife and that she was taking him bread, he refused to have her as a servant. Job's wife then had no choice but to sell her hair for food.

Job's wife had lost everything. She was forced to support Job and herself in a society that gave women few options for employment. She experienced hunger and public humiliation.

When she went out to see Job sitting on the heap of ashes, she cried out in anguish and despair, "Curse God and die" (Job 2:9). Perhaps she was speaking just as much to herself as to her husband.

In the history of the Christian church, Augustine, Calvin, and others have attributed her words to the devil. But I understand them as words of lament—despairing, angry, and helpless words, uttered by one sufferer to another. Her words held at least a glimmer of faith, for in them she acknowledged God's presence and power over life and death. In her position, many of us might have difficulty maintaining enough faith even to be angry at God. Instead, our response to such profound loss might well be one of disbelief and denial: if there is such suffering, then God is dead.

In her pioneering work, *On Death and Dying*, Elisabeth Kubler-Ross outlined five stages of grief: denial, anger, bargaining, depression, and acceptance.[1] She identified these in her interviews with people facing terminal illness, and over the years, these stages have been applied more broadly to anyone facing any kind of grief.

I was already familiar with the Kubler-Ross stages when a new acquaintance suggested them to me as essential grief work. I was surprised at her comment since we had just met, and I immediately felt uneasy. I had never felt angry over my Dearheart's death, but now her comment made me wonder, was I grieving the wrong way? Had I skipped anger as an essential part of grief work? Was her comment meant to warn me that anger was still to come?

Anger

In fact, Kubler-Ross never understood her stages of grief as necessary steps to work through in a linear fashion. In her last book before her death, *On Grief and Grieving*, co-written with David Kessler, she wrote:

> The stages have evolved since their introduction, and they have been very misunderstood over the past three decades. They were never meant to help tuck messy emotions into neat packages. They are responses to loss that many people have, but there is not a typical response to loss, as there is no typical loss. Our grief is as individual as our lives.[2]

Ah, what a relief! Here was permission for me to grieve in my own way—in words penned by none other than the renowned psychiatrist and author of the Kubler-Ross model.

While I didn't feel angry, I had other strong feelings of shock, disappointment, anxiety, guilt, and hurt. Like anger, these other messy emotions found their expression in lament. I needed to cry them out, journal them out, find some way of releasing them.

When Pam Vredevelt and her husband lost their baby halfway to term, she too was a bundle of messy emotions. As much as she wanted to rid herself of her hard feelings, as a counselor, she knew that she needed to feel them. She writes:

> When we are feeling our pain, we are *progressing*. We tend to get mixed up about this process. We think that if we feel pain deeply, we are losing it . . . . Nothing is further

Hope Beyond Our Sorrows

from the truth. When we are feeling, we are moving ahead through the grief process.[3]

Vredevelt encourages her clients to release their anger and other strong emotions in a safe way: in angry talks with God, uncensored journaling, with tears, with a counselor—but with a time limit. Instead of venting for hours on end, she says that therapy sessions are generally kept under an hour for good reason. That's a helpful time frame for working through the painful emotions of grief. Then she suggests deliberately going on to something else to direct attention away from the pain. You might have a cup of tea or do some laundry—anything that will change your focus and redirect your energy.

Anger

HOPE PRACTICE

Do you feel angry? Anxious? Disappointed? Or some other strong emotion? Whatever you feel, give yourself permission to name it. Lament over it. Feel it deeply. Release it through prayer, tears, punching a pillow, or in some other safe way. Whatever you choose, give yourself a time limit of less than an hour. Then refocus your thoughts and emotional energy by vacuuming the stairs, going for a run, weeding the garden, or doing something else constructive.

If you have trouble expressing your messy emotions, read Psalm 77:1–10 as your lament. Cry out with the psalmist: "My whole being refuses to be comforted" (v. 2). Complain aloud to God: "I'm so upset I can't even speak" (v. 4). Ask the hard question: "Has God forgotten how to be gracious?" (v. 9). Let the psalmist's lament be the lament of your heart.

Then notice that all that venting has a limit, for the last ten verses of the psalm turn to praise. If you're ready to join the psalmist's affirmation of faith, read Psalm 77:11–20. Confess with the psalmist: "You are the God who works wonders" (v. 14). If

Hope Beyond Our Sorrows

you're not yet ready for the rest of the psalm, feel free to set it aside for now, and end your time of lament by refocusing your thoughts and emotional energy by listening to music, playing a game, cleaning out the garage, or doing some other physical work.

10

MOURNING

Grieving room is endangered in a culture that thinks it is more helpful to rush past grief than lean into it.
LEANNE FRIESEN, Grieving Room

When my father died suddenly of a heart attack, I helped my mother make arrangements for his funeral. She would talk calmly with the funeral director, and inwardly I would be shouting: *Stop! Stop! This is all wrong! Why are we being so calm and reasonable and polite? My dad has died.* But I didn't say anything out loud, and my mother didn't stop, the funeral director didn't stop, I didn't stop. A minister friend of my dad's would lead the service. One of his best friends would give a tribute.

As a third-generation Canadian, I wasn't familiar with the funeral customs of my Chinese heritage, but I soon learned from my aunts and other older members of my family. After the service, we should have two friends of the family stationed at the door. They were to give each person a white envelope with a piece of candy and a quarter. With my dad's death, we had all experienced bitterness, so we needed something sweet. And the quarter was to be spent on a cup of coffee or something else before returning home. The funeral meal after

Hope Beyond Our Sorrows

the service was to have seven courses, one vegetarian and the others could be favorite foods. But no, the restaurant owner said we should not have chow mein even though it was a family favorite. At the age of seventy-five, my dad's life had been cut short, so long noodles of any kind should not be on the menu.

When my mother passed away years later just a few days short of her eighty-ninth birthday, yes, we could have her favorite Shanghai noodles as part of the funeral meal. "Your mother lived a long, full life," I was told, so the fat, long noodles would be fine. At that time, I also learned about the Chinese custom of observing a period of mourning after the death of a family member. The length of time and specific practices seemed to vary according to one's position in the family and other considerations. But one common practice was for bereaved family members not to visit other people in their homes during the month following a death. Other people could visit the bereaved at the family home. The family could visit with others in a restaurant.

To some that was an outdated custom, rooted in superstition as if a death in the family meant bad luck, so family members should not carry that bad luck to other households. But for me, a time of mourning became a meaningful practice. In the month following my mother's death, I chose not to make any home visits, and I'm grateful for the understanding of my church. I explained it as a period of mourning, as one way to make space for grieving. Instead of rushing around visiting or filling up the empty space, a period of mourning acknowledges and honors the loss. It signals that life has been forever changed, if not for the world at large, then for those who have been affected most deeply.

Mourning

After my Dearheart died, I again observed a period of mourning. COVID-19 pandemic restrictions were beginning to ease, but I decided not to visit people in their homes anyway. I needed to give myself time and space to grieve. To think about my Dearheart and our life together. To pray. To cry. To journal. To go for walks. To listen to his collection of 1980s music. To sort through things and remember. I needed a way to signal that his life and death *mattered*, that life could not—and would not—go on as before, that the world around me would never be the same.

Because my Dearheart died a week and a half before the start of Lent, it seemed fitting for me to observe this period of mourning until Easter Sunday. So when people would ask, Are you open to a new writing assignment? Would you consider volunteering for a committee? Or even, we're having a group over for dinner, and will you join us? I would say I can't even think about that until after Easter. Not that Easter would mean the end of my remembering and praying and doing all of the precious work of grieving, but for at least those few weeks before then, I needed to honor the loss and deliberately leave room to mourn. My mind and heart were so full of grieving that I couldn't think about anything else, and I didn't want to.

During my time of mourning, I took care of the essentials—eating, sleeping, letting people know that my Dearheart was gone. Since there was no in-person funeral, I found other ways to mark his passing and for people to say goodbye. I arranged

Hope Beyond Our Sorrows

for an online tribute with memories from his two brothers and one of his closest friends. I encouraged people to read and add to the tribute, to celebrate my Dearheart's life by giving blood, encouraging a health care worker, doing some other deliberate act of kindness, or giving to a charity of their choice.

I bought a beautiful tea wheel with a variety of colorful, individually wrapped teabags and took it to the nurses at the hospital with a thank you card for all of the care they had shown to my Dearheart and to me. I answered every card I received—from family, friends, members of my church and community. Old high school friends that I hadn't heard from in years sent cards. Even the real estate agent who had helped us buy our townhouse, whom I hadn't seen for over twelve years, sent a card, and thoughtfully included a clipping of the tribute printed in the local newspaper.

"You know you don't have to answer every card," a friend said to me. "Or you could just do them all in a batch the way people send thank you cards for wedding gifts."

"I know," I said. "But I want to. I'm amazed at how many people took the time and made the effort to reach out." I wanted to think about each person, what they had meant to my Dearheart, and what he had meant to them. Besides, without an in-person funeral, there hadn't been a gathering for everyone to come together, so it felt even more important to me to respond personally with a card, an email, a phone call, or in some other way. Even when people would say "no reply necessary," it was a comfort for me to respond, to connect with others who cared, and who shared my grief.

Mourning

HOPE PRACTICE

In his sermon on the mount, Jesus said, "Blessed are those who mourn, for they will be comforted" (Matthew 5:4, NIV). Yet in times of loss, we're sometimes too busy to mourn. When my dad died, there was so much to do that it was only two days later that I realized I had called just one friend. I had been so busy helping my mom with arrangements that I hadn't called on my own support group. I had scarcely tended to my own mourning.

We may sometimes feel that we don't have the luxury of grief. When you've been abruptly let go from your job, you're so busy scrambling for the next one, who has time to mourn? When you've received a difficult diagnosis, you're so preoccupied with medical appointments and what might happen next that it's all you can do to keep going. Besides, the children need their breakfast. The clothes need washing. The bills need paying. Who has time to mourn?

Yet there is wisdom in mourning, in honoring what you've lost instead of too quickly moving on to the next thing. We need time to say goodbye—in more formal ways like a graveside service or a celebration of life, and in more informal ways. So take a

Hope Beyond Our Sorrows

moment now. Choose one or more of the following in memory and honor of your loss: walk, run, or hike, leave an empty chair at the dinner table, take time to look through old photographs, light a candle, wrap yourself in a quilt, put on some music, plan a favorite meal, donate to charity, plant a tree, consider other ways to remember and mourn.

PART TWO

Middle Grief
A Hard Path

11

WHILE IT WAS
STILL DARK

God is always a God of surprises.
N.T. WRIGHT, *Surprised by Hope*

Easter Sunday, two months and a day after my Dearheart died, my church sang Charles Wesley's great hymn:

Christ the Lord is ris'n today, Alleluia!
All creation joins to say, Alleluia!
Raise your joys and triumphs high, Alleluia!
Sing oh heav'ns and earth reply, Alleluia![1]

How fitting that each line celebrates the resurrection of Jesus with Alleluia, which means praise the Lord!

Only Charles Wesley didn't write the hymn that way. Years after he wrote the verses, an unknown editor added the Alleluias to Wesley's original text, most likely to complement the stirring music. Today I can't imagine the song without those Alleluias, for they add an extra note of joy to this wonderful Easter hymn celebrating the risen Christ.

But when we came to that hymn on the first Easter Sunday after my Dearheart's death, I can't say that I was filled with resurrection joy. I was still grieving. I could hardly sing and gave myself permission not to; instead, I let myself be carried by the voices of the congregation around me. I felt the weight of my Dearheart's loss and deeply missed him worshiping beside me. I thought of that first Easter morning when Jesus rose from the dead, and realized that it, too, began with the weight of loss.

The gospel of John begins the Easter story this way:

> Early in the morning of the first day of the week, while it was still dark, Mary Magdalene came to the tomb and saw that the stone had been taken away from the tomb.
> —John 20:1

Mary had started out from her home while it was still dark. Just as she had wanted to be near Jesus in his suffering on the cross, she wanted to be near Jesus even in his death. So she rose early to go to the place where Jesus was buried. By the time Mary got to the garden, it was just light enough so she could see that the stone had been removed—and that Jesus' body was gone. The tomb was empty.

Jesus had already risen from the dead! Somehow while it was still dark and while there were no witnesses, God had raised Jesus to new life. That's how God's resurrection power works—while it's still dark, in secret when no one's looking, in ways that we don't expect.

But Mary didn't know all of that yet. She only knew that the tomb was empty. Jesus was gone from her life, and now even his body was gone from the tomb. In her tears and confusion,

While It Was Still Dark

when she later saw Jesus in the garden, she assumed he was the gardener.

Jesus didn't rush to correct her. Instead, he gently asked her, "Why are you crying?" (John 20:15). He began with the weight of Mary's loss and misery. He accepted her tears. He did not try to talk her out of crying. He did not say things are not as bad they seem. He didn't even rush to tell her the good news of his resurrection.

Instead, Jesus began by acknowledging Mary's despair, and only after that did he reveal who he was by calling her by name. Only then did she recognize him and the power of his resurrection. Only then did her tears of grief become tears of joy, and Mary could announce to the rest of the disciples, "I've seen the Lord" (John 20:18).

In the depths of Mary's grief, Jesus had called her by name and brought her new life. That's how God's resurrection power works! While it's still dark, when we're numb with grief, when confusion reigns, when tears blur our vision, God is at work to bring new life and renew our joy.

The Easter story is at the core of Christian faith: Christ is risen! It's surprising and miraculous. It's full of hope. It's worthy of praise. The weight of the cross, the weight of suffering and death is finally lifted and gives way to glorious light and life.

This is also a great mystery. I don't know how it happened. None of us knows. We all have a long way to go in understanding death and resurrection, life and faith. But even when we can't understand the mystery, God's resurrection power

Hope Beyond Our Sorrows

is at work. The resurrection of Jesus and his encounter with Mary give me hope.

When I am in the depths of grief, when I'm in no mood for resurrection joy even on an Easter Sunday, when I have trouble recognizing Jesus' presence in my life, even then God's resurrection power is still at work, while it's still dark.

Then the risen Christ comes to meet me—in prayer, in Scripture, in silence, in music, in worship, in connection and community with others, in so many ways. The risen Christ comes to meet us—wherever we are, in whatever grief or confusion or questions or trials we face. Our sorrows are met with compassion, our names gently called, and God's resurrection power unfolds in us new life—and yes, even joy.

While It Was Still Dark
HOPE PRACTICE

Easter Sunday the following year—one year and seven weeks after my Dearheart died—I was more able to sing with the rest of the congregation: "Christ the Lord is ris'n today, Alleliua!" Once again I could join in with "Praise the Lord!"

Yet even in my early grief, when I found it hard to sing Alleluia, music was still very much a part of my journey. Music helped me pour out my heart to God. I listened to "Healer of Our Every Ill" and other hymns, to Canadian singer/songwriter Laura Smith's "Safe Home, Sweet Light," Justin Bieber's Top 10 hit "Ghost," written with singer/songwriter Jon Bellion, who missed his grandmother. Whether or not these were first written as prayers, they gave voice to mine.

At other times, music was a welcome distraction from my sad thoughts. I listened to my Dearheart's collection of the Beatles, Billy Joel, and other artists while I did the dishes or folded laundry. I played the piano in my own stumbling way, passing over music with too many sharps or flats in favor of less complicated pieces.

You may also find music a helpful companion on your journey. If a song or other piece of music comes to you immediately, ask

Hope Beyond Our Sorrows

yourself, How does this relate to my grief? Does it give voice to my prayers? Serve as a companion in my sorrow? Allow me to vent my frustration, anger, or other strong emotion? Distract me from negative thoughts? Consider putting together your own playlist.

Feel free to listen, to sing or not sing, to play or not play, just once or over and over as many times as you wish. If you need distracting, let the music distract you. If you need comfort, let the music carry you and your grief nearer to the heart of God. Know that God is with you. Know that even now, hidden where you cannot see it, new life is unfolding and new joy awaits.

12

THE JOURNEY OF GRIEF

Loss is not an easy road to walk.
JOAN CHITTISTER, *The Story of Ruth*

In my mother's final days, I sat at her bedside and read aloud through the pilgrimage songs of the Bible, Psalms 120–134. Originally written for ancient pilgrims travelling to the temple, these psalms also address our journey through life. They speak of family and community, work and rest, suffering and rejoicing, grief and goodness, sin and God's mercy, lament and worship, waiting, peace, and so much more.

> I raise my eyes toward the mountains.
>> Where will my help come from?
> —Psalm 121:1

> I cry out to you from the depths, LORD—
> my Lord, listen to my voice!
> —Psalm 130:1–2

> Lift up your hands to the sanctuary
>> and bless the LORD!
> May the LORD, the maker of heaven and earth,
>> bless you from Zion.
> —Psalm 134:2–3

I sat and read through all fifteen pilgrimage songs as prayers for my mother, for myself, and for all of us walking through that valley of the shadow of death. I prayed the psalms would speak comfort to her even as she continued to sleep peacefully and did not respond. At least the sound of my voice in her otherwise quiet room did me some good, with the words of the psalms bearing witness to God's presence and goodness.

In the ancient world, those who worshiped at the temple in Jerusalem would travel there at least three times a year for different religious festivals. They would come from all the surrounding villages, and because travel in the ancient world could be dangerous, they would usually travel in groups. Before they set out on their journey—and all along the way—they would often read or sing one of the pilgrimage psalms and pray together. As pilgrims, they knew where they were going: to the temple in Jerusalem. And since they made the trip several times a year, they knew the way.

This past year, I learned about a different kind of pilgrimage that doesn't have a specific destination or a particular route. Instead, the pilgrim sets out on a journey, not knowing where it will lead, but trusting in God's guidance and direction along the way. This practice of *peregrination* comes from the tradition of Celtic Christianity and a sixth-century Irish monk known as Brendan the Voyager. St. Brendan's ministry took him to the Scottish Islands and throughout Ireland, where he established a number of monasteries. Legends tell of him traveling even more widely, perhaps as far as Iceland and even

The Journey of Grief

Canada. He set sail, not knowing where he was going, but trusting in God's Spirit to guide him.

For me, the journey of grief is more peregrination than pilgrimage. In grief, I don't know where I am going, or how I'm going to get there. How will I navigate the rough waters around me? How will I keep afloat in the wind and storms? Will I find good harbor? Is there even a destination? Without my travelling companion, my Dearheart, I feel that I've lost my way. I no longer know the direction of my dreams.

A small business owner who had fallen behind on his rent and other expenses had to close his store. He lost his dream of owning his own business. He lost his investment. And he also lost his pride and sense of self-esteem, which he says took him years to regain. A young mother says that after her son died, she realized that she had lost her son, she lost the future they would have had together, and she lost herself. She felt overwhelmed, anxious, confused, as if she no longer knew who she was, where she was going, or what she should do next.

As fellow grievers, we're on a journey, a peregrination. Destination: unknown. Itinerary: unknown. But perhaps we can learn from St. Brendan the Voyager. When he left on his legendary journey to travel across the ocean to places unknown, he did not go by himself. Another fourteen monks helped pack the boat with provisions and planned to go with him. When another three monks asked to join, he welcomed them on board too.

At one point on their seafaring voyage, the waves and weather grew strangely calm. Even when they worked the oars

Hope Beyond Our Sorrows

as hard as they could, they made no progress and remained adrift in the middle of the ocean. "Fear not," St. Brendan said to them, "for our God will be a helper, a mariner, and a pilot for us. Take in the oars and keep the sails set, so that God may guide us."[1]

Like St. Brendan and his companions, in the peregrination of our grief, we may not know where we're going or how we'll get there, but we too can look to God for guidance. In stormy weather and strange calm, our God is our helper and pilot.

The Journey of Grief

HOPE PRACTICE

Choose one or more of the following questions to reflect on the peregrination of your grief:

- What provisions do you need for this journey?
- Who will help you pack and accompany you?
- What does it mean for you to keep your sails set, so God may guide you?

You may find it helpful to write down any answers that come to you. If the questions raise further questions for you, feel free to write those down. Or if you feel so lost that you can't think and keep drawing a blank, then just sit quietly for a moment. Rest assured, that sense of not knowing the answers—or not even understanding the questions—is part of peregrination. Just as St. Brendan and his companions relied on God to guide them, we can rely on God to guide us too as we continue the journey.

Hope Beyond Our Sorrows

A Prayer for the Journey
Attributed to St. Brendan

Help me to journey beyond the familiar
and into the unknown.
Give me the faith to leave old ways
and break fresh ground with You.
Christ of the mysteries, I trust You
to be stronger than each storm within me.
I will trust in the darkness and know
that my times, even now, are in Your hand.
Tune my spirit to the music of heaven,
and somehow, make my obedience count for You.[2]

13

THE LOSSES WE CARRY

Grief is heavy. Carrying its weight is tiring.
BOB DEITS, *Life After Loss*

When it comes to life-changing loss, some speak of primary and secondary losses. So if you lose your job, that's your primary loss. But besides the loss of your actual work and paycheck, you may also experience related secondary losses: the loss of work friends, the loss of your role and sense of identity, a loss of confidence, a loss of structure to your days and weeks. With the death of a spouse, secondary losses might include the loss of financial stability, the loss of companionship, the loss of retirement dreams, and more.

These losses are secondary because they occur as a result of a primary loss. They sometimes go unrecognized until after the initial shock wears off, after some time has passed and in the midst of daily responsibilities. But although they may occur later, although we might call them secondary in that sense, they are still a significant source of pain and grief. There is nothing secondary about that.

When Job and his wife lost their children in the earthquake, that was a primary loss. But they also lost the grandchildren that they might have had one day. When their servants and animals were taken and killed, that was a primary loss. But they also lost their ability to support themselves, they lost standing in their community, they lost hope. These primary and secondary losses were closely related, and each was significant.

My Dearheart's death was a primary loss, but it meant many other secondary losses as well. Without him, I had to learn how to put air in my car tires when they got too low. I bought a little stepladder so I could change the light bulbs that I couldn't reach on my own. I learned to turn off the water to our outdoor faucets so they wouldn't freeze in the winter. I went alone to our high school reunion. These changes all represent secondary losses related to my Dearheart's passing: the loss of his partnership in running our household, the loss of our shared high school history, the loss of his companionship on social occasions.

In his book, *Life After Loss*, author Bob Deits credits his wife for noting "the stacking nature of loss."[1] Such secondary losses stack up under the primary loss. Secondary losses are not separate, but very much part of any life-changing loss we experience.

Miriam Neff cared for her husband for three years before his death from amyotrophic lateral sclerosis (ALS). During those years of caregiving, their friends would call regularly, stop by to visit, bring meals, and offer support in other ways. When she read that widows often lose 75 percent of their friends, she didn't believe that would happen to her. But to her sad surprise, it became true for her as well.

Some friends couldn't understand what she was going through, and how she was changing. After caring for her husband and being his advocate in the health care system, she had become more outspoken. Some of her interests had also changed, so those friendships built around common interests were no longer a good match. She wrote, "During my first year alone, the exit of friends has been one of the more painful parts of my journey."[2] The loss of her husband was intensified by the secondary, stacked loss of their friends.

When a pastor is forced out of the church, Cheryl Berto says that "it is probably best understood as a divorce rather than a job loss."[3] Besides the loss of employment, income, and any housing that may have been provided, there is the loss of community for pastor, spouse, and any children. The loss of friends. A loss of confidence in the church or in any church. Even perhaps a loss of faith.

For members of a congregation who leave their church under difficult circumstances, the losses also stack up. Besides the primary loss of church membership, there may also be the secondary loss of friends, the loss of a sense of home, the loss of related denominational relationships. Some find it difficult even to enter their former church building for a wedding or a funeral. Some struggle to find a new church home anywhere else.

Sometimes loss stacks up in other ways—not as related secondary losses, but as multiple losses happening at the same time or in quick succession. In her book, *When Grief Descends*, Anne

Hope Beyond Our Sorrows

Mackie Morelli describes an especially hard season of life for her and her family. In the course of six years, her mother lost her home in a severe flood, and a number of different family members were diagnosed with multiple sclerosis, cancer, dementia, post-traumatic stress, and other mental health and chronic illnesses. During those same years, her mother and father died. Her mother-in-law and sister-in-law died.

Her own health suffered, and she writes, "As our losses accumulated, my grief shifted into complex trauma. Oftentimes, the grief was suffocating. It felt like I had to struggle to draw the next breath."[4]

The Losses We Carry

HOPE PRACTICE

Losses accumulate. Grief accumulates. In the first few months after my Dearheart's death, the losses stacked up for me too. I had lost my Dearheart as the first reader and responder for much of my writing, as my traveling partner, and the co-author of our shared dreams and goals for the future. Two months after my Dearheart's passing, I spoke at the celebration of life for one of our church members who had also been a mentor and friend to both of us. I'm grateful that I didn't lose other friends during that time due to death or drifting away, but I can understand how painful the loss of friends can be. While it may be considered a "secondary" loss, the pain is just as real and valid as any other loss.

Take a moment to list the losses that have accumulated for you. Some might come to mind immediately: the death of a loved one and all the related losses, the loss of relationships through divorce, the loss of a job or a church. What are the secondary losses that you might not have considered: the loss of sleep, the loss of appetite, the loss of friends, the loss of dreams for the future, and more?

Hope Beyond Our Sorrows

What losses do you tend to dismiss as lesser losses? One woman scolded herself for being upset over the death of her cat. A man who relocated from one city to another for a better job couldn't understand why he felt bad about moving away—after all he had wanted to move. But his move for positive reasons also meant the loss of his previous co-workers, the loss of his favorite coffee shop, the loss of so much that was familiar to him, and these losses brought their own grief.

As you reflect on these and other losses, offer them up in prayer. Receive the invitation of Jesus: "Come to me, all you who are struggling hard and carrying heavy loads, and I will give you rest" (Matthew 11:28).

Then offer this response: I come to you, Jesus, with the weight of these losses: some are fresh burdens, some long-standing; I've counted some as greater, some lesser; but now I name and recognize each one. I commit each one to your hands, and receive your gift of rest.

14

WHEN ONE STEP FEELS LIKE TOO MUCH

If you haven't lost someone close to you, you may not realize how big grief actually is, how hard it is to unearth yourself from the mess its presence makes in your life.
CLARISSA MOLL, *Beyond the Darkness*

For me, the journey of grief was not a pilgrimage since I didn't know where I was going. Nor was it an orderly peregrination moving forward step by step. I couldn't seem to find a path, so my steps were this way and that way, in fits and starts, and I often felt too stunned to move. How could I possibly be on a journey when even one step felt like too much?

When people talked about doing death work, getting things done, and checking things off a list, I felt lost. I had so many lists: two lists from the hospital social worker, another list from the funeral home, another list from the credit union, each list pages long and overwhelming. Plus each thing listed was never just one thing, but a cluster of many different things.

"Cancel what needs to be canceled" meant finding my Dearheart's driver's licence, passport, credit cards, and multiple other cards and memberships for this and that, deciding if they needed to be canceled or changed to my name, finding

99

the contact information, emailing or phoning, being patient with staff who were unsympathetic or didn't know what to do. One morning, to deal with just one piece of paperwork, I was on the phone for over two and a half hours, much of that time on hold or being transferred from one department to another and another and another. I needed the rest of the day to recover from the frustration of that one thing—and I still had to call back two weeks later before the issue was finally resolved!

What's more, the various lists given to me didn't include everything. What was I to do with my Dearheart's online presence? With his website on perspective criticism, his animated video course for learning New Testament Greek, his book contracts? Those, too, were on my heart and mind, in one big jumble along with all of the other to-dos and my swirl of thoughts and emotions.

So instead of an orderly list, I had a huge, swirling ball of random things. Every so often I would brace myself, snatch one thing out of the chaos, do what I could with it, then throw it back to continue swirling until the next time. No wonder I felt overwhelmed.

A reader once suggested that I write a few thoughts "for when you or a loved one feel overwhelmed by life." She had asked for this well before my Dearheart's recurrence of cancer, well before his sudden passing. In response, I had written a number of posts on lessons I had learned in the often too-busy thick and thin of life and ministry. Now I was relearning those same lessons in my new season of grief and loss.

When One Step Feels Like Too Much

Let the overwhelming flood wash over you. Instead of panicking and desperately flailing around to get out of the chaos, let yourself be overwhelmed. Life is overwhelming, grief is overwhelming, and it's okay to feel that way. When you feel paralyzed, don't pressure yourself to act. Just breathe. Do the essentials, and leave the rest. Be gentle with yourself, and with those around you. Take a nap if you can. Eat from your sad food group.

Remind yourself that feeling overwhelmed is not a 9-1-1 emergency. It's okay if you have more questions than answers about your life. It's okay if you can't resolve everything in the swirling mass before you. Even when your circumstances are definitely not okay, even when you've had a life-changing loss, whatever overwhelms you, God is greater.

Practice the fine art of knowing what can wait. When I was in high school, one Saturday morning I remember my mother saying to me, "The beds can wait—let's go shopping!" I don't know what we were shopping for or why it was suddenly so important, but her words have stayed with me. Over the years, I've learned that lesson well—not so much about shopping, but about knowing what can wait.

So when I was told I didn't have to change the title on our townhouse unless I was planning to sell, I decided to wait. When I was told I didn't have to change our car registration until the insurance was due, again I decided to wait. That relieved some pressure so I could attend to some of the more pressing things, and beyond that, I could give myself grace just to be in the present moment.

Lean on God. In times of stress or when we're feeling overwhelmed, God may seem far away or indifferent to our circumstances. We may feel too overwhelmed for prayer or

Hope Beyond Our Sorrows

Scripture, too restless for meeting God in silence. We might question our faith. Such responses to grief are not uncommon. In those times when leaning on God may seem too difficult or even impossible, we can let ourselves be carried by the prayers of others. Let others bear our burdens and lift us up. That's part of what it means to be in Christian community.

At other times, we might find ourselves surprised by the presence of God. During my Dearheart's struggle with cancer, I would often spontaneously pray, "Make haste to help us, O God." The words came to me unbidden and so often that I looked them up and discovered that they were a variation on Psalm 38:22: "Make haste to help me, O Lord" (KJV). I don't recall memorizing that verse or preaching on it, but somehow those words had worked themselves into my soul and resurfaced when I needed them. After my Dearheart's passing and even today, I still find myself praying, "Make haste to help me, O God."

Lean on others. Do you have a family member or good friend that you can lean on? A sister or brother in the church? A counselor, pastor, or spiritual director to talk to? When you feel too overwhelmed to pray, it's a gift to have others pray for you. When you're overwhelmed by daily living, it's a blessing to have people in your life who can watch your children for the afternoon, or bring you a meal, or help out in some other practical way.

I wish that were true for everyone all of the time. But not all of us have friends and families like that, and even those of us who do may find that the people we thought we could count on are not always there for us. Sometimes they too are overwhelmed by life, or preoccupied with other things, or simply unable to respond. As we seek to be gentle with ourselves, we may need to be gentle with others too.

True confession, I still haven't done all of the things on all of the lists that I received after my Dearheart's death. Yes, I eventually transferred the townhouse title even though I still don't have plans to sell and move. I transferred the car registration when I renewed the insurance. But there are still a few things left in his name alone because they were too cumbersome to change, and I still haven't figured out what to do with some of his online presence. For some who grieve, I realize that such lack of closure would be troubling, and if that's your situation, by all means, keep working to get things done. But if you're feeling overwhelmed, be encouraged by the knowledge that some things can wait.

When One Step Feels Like Too Much

HOPE PRACTICE

In Scripture, the Psalms are full of waiting. At various times, the psalmists speak of waiting for help (Psalm 38), for wisdom and forgiveness (Psalm 39), for rescue (Psalm 40), for morning and redemption (Psalm 130). And whatever the particular circumstances of their waiting, in all things, the psalmists clearly "wait for the Lord" (Psalm 31:24; 37:7; 130:6–7).

So, too, as we wait for the overwhelming flood to subside, as we follow through on those tasks that can't wait and set aside those that can, as we lean on other people in our lives, in a larger sense we also wait for God. We wait for God's power to protect and provide for us. We wait for God's presence to sustain us. We wait for God's mercy to bring us safely home.

Sit with these words for some moments:

So now, Lord, what should I be waiting for?
[*Take your time with this question, and write down any answers that come to you. Let them wait for you on the page.*]
My hope is set on you.
[*Commit those things that you are waiting for to God.*]
—Psalm 39:7

15

A PLACE TO START

The LORD will protect you on your journeys—whether going or coming—from now until forever from now.
PSALM 121:8

When my Dearheart and I got married, our pastor gave us this verse:

Whither thou goest, I will go; and where thou lodgest,
I will lodge:
thy people shall be my people, and thy God my God.
—Ruth 1:16 (KJV)

Those words seemed like a good starting point for us as a young couple—to commit ourselves to make a home together, to become family to one another, and above all to hold on to God. Over the years, they became our story as we made a home together in and around Vancouver, British Columbia, then spent four years in the United States before moving back to Canada and the Fraser Valley.

Yet now as I look back on these words of Scripture—celebrated with joy at our wedding and so joyfully lived out—I realize how sad and desperate they were in their original setting. At this point in Ruth's story, her husband had died, her father-in-law had died, and her mother-in-law wanted to send Ruth back to her birth family in Moab. But Ruth begged her mother-in-law not to send her away. These words formed part of her desperate plea. Instead of bringing shame on her family and burdening them with an unexpected mouth to feed, Ruth wanted to go with Naomi—to make a new home with her in Judah, to embrace a new people, and to continue following the God she had come to know.

Unlike Ruth, when my Dearheart died, I did not have to go live with other family members or move out of my home. I had food to eat in my cupboards and fridge, and could easily go to the grocery store for more as needed. I had my people—not living in the same household, but supportive family members and friends and church that I knew I could count on. Yet like Ruth without her husband, I, too, faced what felt like an uncertain future.

Maybe you feel that way too over the death of a loved one. Over a broken marriage. Or a difficult relationship with a son or daughter. A deep disappointment in your work life, in a friendship, in your church life. Whatever loss we face, the future may seem uncertain. Yet, like Ruth and Naomi, perhaps we can find a new place to begin.

To escape famine in their own country, Naomi, her husband, and their two sons had moved from their home in Judah to Moab. After some years, Naomi's husband died, and ten years later, their two adult sons died. So Naomi and her two Moabite daughters-in-law, Ruth and Orpah, were left as widows to fend for themselves.

A Place to Start

Without her husband, without her sons, and in a foreign land, Naomi had no one and nothing to fall back on. No male relatives to provide for her and protect her in the patriarchal culture of ancient Moab. No job or pension or social assistance that might be possible in our day. How would she survive?

Naomi decided to return to Judah, where the famine was over. She and her husband still had relatives there, and in Judah, widows and others living in poverty were allowed to glean grain from the edges of the fields. The religious law recognized the needs of widows along with orphans and immigrants, as they were all economically and socially vulnerable (Deuteronomy 14:29; 16:11, 14; 24:17, 19–21; 26:12–13). The prophet Isaiah pronounced God's judgement on those who "deprive the needy of their rights . . . rob the poor . . . make widows their loot . . . steal from orphans!" (Isaiah 10:2). In contrast, God received praise as the "father of orphans and defender of widows" (Psalm 68:5), who enacts justice on their behalf (Deuteronomy 10:18).

For Naomi, Judah was home. She would have access to food, the shelter of the religious law, and the potential of supportive relationships. God would protect and defend her. She could rebuild her life, and may even have felt relieved when Ruth insisted on going with her. It would be better for the two women to travel together than for Naomi to journey alone from Moab to Judah.

When they arrived in Bethlehem, the women of the town wondered, could this really be Naomi? She and her family had left Judah full of dreams for their future together, but now this broken woman stood before them with only her daughter-in-law at her side. Naomi replied:

> Don't call me Naomi [which means *pleasant*], but call me Mara,
> [which means *bitter*] for the Almighty has made me very bitter.
> I went away full, but the LORD has returned me empty.
> —Ruth 1:20–21

Naomi lamented over her situation, and we might say with good reason. She had lost her husband and two sons, so why should anyone expect her to be *pleasant*? She didn't feel pleasant at all; instead, she felt bitter. Grief had changed her. She didn't try to justify her harsh feelings. She didn't try to hide them or explain them away. Instead, she openly expressed her grief among the women in her community and before God.

Naomi and Ruth had taken the risk of traveling from Moab to Judah, crossing the fifty rugged miles on foot and not knowing how they might be received once they arrived. For them, the risk had been well worth it. They had needed food and a support system, a community and a safe place to express their grief. So they had taken steps to find those things. In their season of grief, they had practiced healthy self-care—not as self-indulgence, but as part of rebuilding their lives.

Another story of resilience and God's provision appears in 2 Kings 4:1–7. A woman had lost her husband and then fallen into such deep debt that she was about to lose her children. Since she couldn't repay what she owed, her creditor threatened

A Place to Start

to take her children away as slaves. Her husband had been a prophet, so she turned to the prophet Elisha for help. What was she to do? All she had left was a small jar of oil.

Elisha told her to collect as many empty containers as she could from her neighbors, return home with her children, and behind closed doors to start pouring the little oil she had into the containers. She filled one after another and another, and for as many containers as she and her children had collected, the oil kept flowing. God worked a miracle with ordinary oil, ordinary household jars, and ordinary people! She could sell the oil, pay her debts with the proceeds, save her children, and save herself.

I sometimes wonder, if the woman had borrowed fewer containers, would God have given her less oil? If the neighbors had refused to lend them, would God have still met her need? In this story, it seems that God chose to limit divine power and to work instead through human action and human compassion. Once there were no more empty containers, there was also no more oil.

It may be tempting to interpret this story narrowly in spiritual terms. God satisfies our spiritual hunger and thirst, we might say. When we are lonely and in need, God reaches out to touch us. It's true that God meets our inner and hidden needs with divine love and provision. In this story of the prophet's widow, God met her spiritual needs—comforting her in her mourning and giving her strength to care for her children. And God intervened to provide for her physical needs as well, working through Elisha who advised her, through her neighbors who gave their empty containers, her children who collected them and helped with pouring the oil, and through the woman's willingness to act.

A Place to Start

HOPE PRACTICE

The unnamed widow in danger of losing her children had an obvious and pressing need. If you and your family have an obvious and pressing need, you have most likely already appealed to any Elishas that you know and asked for help from other family members and neighbors. You have most likely already explored options through your church and community agencies, and have been praying for God to make a way for you. If you're still working at these things and more, please know that you are showing amazing resilience, and I do not want to add to your burden. I pray that God would continue to strengthen and restore you, to work in you and through you and beyond you to meet your needs and the needs of your family.

In my early and middle grief, when I felt stuck and struggled to break free, I didn't always know what I needed. So for me it was helpful to take a step back and look at the big picture, to consider all aspects of life: thoughts and feelings, work and finances, legal issues, managing the household, managing stress, having a network of support. If you're not sure what you need, consider your own physical, financial, mental, emotional, social, and spiritual

A Place to Start

well-being. Who are your Elishas? Who are your neighbors, not necessarily the people who live next door to you, but the people that you can count on to help you?

O God, who worked a miracle for this unnamed widow, we are grateful for the witness of Scripture, for the care you have shown to widows, orphans, immigrants, and other vulnerable people. Yet there are still many today in need of a miracle. Sometimes we need to be the neighbor willing to share what we have with others. Sometimes we're the ones in need, called to take what little we have and pour it out. May that be our starting place, caring for others and practicing healthy self-care. May we respond in faith and hope as you fill our empty vessels, multiply our meager resources, and make a miracle.

16

ONE FOOT IN FRONT
OF THE OTHER

One small step, one deep breath, at a time.
KATE BOWLER and **JESSICA RICHIE,** *The Lives We Actually Have*

A number of years ago, my Dearheart and I received a calendar with inspirational sayings. "Recognize the possibilities and embrace them with courage and confidence." "It's OK to fail. If you're not failing, you're not growing." "Endurance is not just the ability to bear a hard thing, but to turn it into glory." The source of each quote was unidentified, but I looked up this last one, and discovered that it was attributed to the Scottish minister, professor, and author William Barclay.

Of course, I thought. William Barclay was well-known for his popular commentaries. I had used several of them in preparing for sermons, and had always appreciated his clarity and creative use of language. But what many people might not know about the prolific writer is that he and his wife had a daughter who died when she was just twenty-one years old. Their daughter and the young man that she might have married one day were both drowned in a tragic boating accident.

Hope Beyond Our Sorrows

How did the Barclays endure that difficult season? In a radio interview, Barclay said that while God did not stop their daughter's accident, God stilled the storm in their hearts. That's how he and his wife were able to endure the agony of their daughter's death.

In *A Spiritual Autobiography*, he wrote:

> When things like that happen, there are just three things to be said. First, to understand them is impossible. Second, Jesus does not offer us solutions to them. What he does offer us is his strength and help somehow to accept what we cannot understand. Third, the one fatal reaction is the bitter resentment which for ever after meets life with a chip on the shoulder and a grudge against God. The one saving reaction is simply to go on living, to go on working, and to find in the presence of Jesus Christ the strength and courage to meet life with steady eyes, and to know the comfort that God too is afflicted in my affliction.[1]

That's the endurance to bear the hard thing and turn it into glory. For William Barclay, that wasn't just an inspirational saying for a calendar. For him and his wife, it was a daily practice as they responded to their daughter's death, to go on living, to go on working, to go on trusting in God.

On the deaths of her husband and two sons, Naomi also endured deep grief. Yet she too continued to go on living, working, and relying on God. She literally put one foot in front of the other to make the journey from Moab to Judah. She made a new home for herself and reconnected with extended family

One Foot in Front of the Other

members and her community. She encouraged her daughter-in-law and offered her wise counsel. The two became so close that for most of the book of Ruth, Naomi called Ruth not "daughter-in-law" but "daughter."

Ruth had also endured the loss of her husband, and like Naomi, she too continued to live, work, and trust in God. Traveling with her mother-in-law from Moab to Judah, Ruth also literally put one foot in front of the other, but for her the trip was not a homecoming. For her, Judah was a foreign land, but she went on to make it her home. Encouraged by Naomi, she went to work in the fields where she was met with kindness from other workers and from the owner, who was a relative of her late father-in-law. She and Boaz married, and she went on to give birth to a son, a grandson for Naomi, whom they named Obed.

The two women got on with their lives, and their story ended with blessing as the community of women surrounded Naomi and blessed the Lord for her new grandson: "He will restore your life and sustain you in your old age. Your daughter-in-law who loves you has given birth to him" (Ruth 4:15). In a traditional culture with few opportunities for women to support themselves, they envisioned Naomi's grandson growing up to support her. But by giving Naomi a grandson, it was really God who restored Naomi's life and sustained her in her old age. And what no one knew was that the birth of Obed would one day lead to the birth of Jesus, the Savior of the world. The endurance of Naomi and Ruth would truly turn into glory.

Hope Beyond Our Sorrows

Daniel also learned to put one foot in front of the other, to continue living, working, and trusting God in a season of great trouble. When King Nebuchadnezzar of Babylon captured the city of Jerusalem, he brought Daniel and some of the other young men to serve in his royal court. But for all his power, King Nebuchadnezzar was a troubled man. He could hardly sleep, and when he did sleep, he had disturbing dreams.

So the king called the wise men of Babylon together and demanded that they tell him his dream. But the wise men protested—the task was impossible. At that, the king flew into a rage and ordered them all to be executed, including Daniel and his companions. But Daniel spoke up, asked for some time, and told the king he would tell him the dream and interpret it.

Daniel put his trust in God, and that night, God revealed the king's dream to him. The next day, Daniel told the king his dream and what it meant. Then Daniel and all of the wise men of Babylon were saved from death.

But Daniel himself had some terrible dreams. In one there seemed to be four beasts at war. In another, a ram and a goat. The imagery was so vivid and so terrifying that Daniel said he "was overwhelmed and felt sick for days" (Daniel 8:27a). But after those days, Daniel—though still troubled by his dreams— "got up and went about the king's business" (Daniel 8:27b). Instead of continuing to obsess over the dreams he could not understand, he too put one foot in front of the other and got on with life.

So too, for us who grieve, we may be heartsick and overcome for some days as Daniel was. But then, we too can get on with life by putting one foot in front of the other. We can get on with the king's business, so to speak, with whatever God has placed before us.

One Foot in Front of the Other

HOPE PRACTICE

When I'm overwhelmed mentally, emotionally, spiritually, physically, it can be hard to get on with the next step, or even to know what the next step might be. Chaos seems to have the upper hand. To regain a sense of order, I find it helps to put one foot in front of the other and start with something physical.

That might mean going outside to look at the garden or taking a walk around the block. Or when getting out the door feels like too much, I might start instead with something indoors. Like gathering the dishes that have been left in the living room, the bedroom, downstairs, and everywhere, and at least getting them all into the kitchen. Clearing the bags of recycling away from the front door and stashing them in the garage. It may seem trivial, but somehow as I put my physical environment in order, I start feeling less overwhelmed and more able to chip away at some of the bigger challenges I face.

Consider how you might put one foot in front of the other today. Do something physical outdoors. Or start indoors. Make your bed for a change. Clear off the kitchen counter. Declutter just one shelf instead of the entire closet. If you're dealing with

Hope Beyond Our Sorrows

mental illness and overwhelmed beyond self-help solutions, you might start by calling your therapist or doctor.

Above all, take heart from the examples of William Barclay, Naomi and Ruth, and Daniel. Remember that there is sorrow too in the heart of God, who is afflicted in our affliction. Let us turn to Jesus, "a man of sorrows, and acquainted with grief" (Isaiah 53:3 KJV). Let us put one foot in front of the other and move in faith with the Spirit who goes before us.

17

WISDOM ALONG
THE WAY

*When someone you love dies, everything gets mixed up;
you experience a conflict of emotions: grief, loss, self-pity,
love, compassion. You must also deal with the reactions
of others.*

SHARON BUTALA, *Where I Live Now*

A week and a half after my Dearheart's sudden passing, I was scheduled to begin teaching a six-week online course on Sabbath as a lifelong, life-giving rhythm. My course was part of an adult enrichment program, and participants had already registered. I had already been preparing. Months earlier, when I had been invited to teach, my Dearheart had encouraged me to say yes. But now without him, my heart wasn't in it. How could I possibly keep that commitment when all I wanted to do was lie down and cry?

As I lamented over this with a good friend, she shared my grief and patiently listened. Then she gave me some wise advice in the form of a question: Why not ask to start the course a week later? Perhaps if I had been thinking straight I would have thought of that myself, but in my muddle of grief, her words were a revelation to me. As soon as she said them, I felt a wave of relief.

Throughout my Dearheart's health challenges, he had always encouraged me to continue writing, speaking, and teaching. "People need to hear your voice," he would say, and the tasks and rhythm of ministry grounded us both in the midst of the chaos of Covid and cancer. "It will be good for you to get back to work," my friend said to me, and I knew my Dearheart would think so too.

When I contacted the director of the program, he expressed his shock and sympathy and readily agreed to a delayed start for my course. From my previous teaching, I knew many of those registered, some of whom had been aware of our situation and had been praying for us. By the time the course started, I was feeling more composed, buoyed by the knowledge that the class would be more like meeting with friends than strangers, and ready to teach in my Dearheart's honor.

In just this one example, I'm grateful for the many positive interactions I've had with other people. From my good friend who listened and gently offered wise counsel, to the program director who responded with sympathy and a willingness to accommodate me, to the participants who shifted their schedules for the delayed start, gladly received me, and shared in our discussion and practice of Sabbath. In my time of mourning, teaching that course became so life-giving for me that our time together each week seemed like a welcome Sabbath.

Unfortunately for Job as he grieved his devastating loss, the reactions of those around him were not always so positive. His

Wisdom Along the Way

wife was so caught up in her own grief that she had no words to comfort him. Three of his closest friends had started well by coming to mourn with Job. They wept over him. They tore their robes and scattered dust as traditional signs of deep grief. They sat with him in silence. But once they started talking, they seemed to be more critical than supportive.

Their conversation goes on for most of the book of Job, with his friends arguing and Job trying to defend himself. At one point, Job accuses God, "I cry to you, and you don't answer" (Job 30:20). But after a while, God answers Job and asks a series of pointed questions: "Did you give strength to the horse, clothe his neck with a mane, cause him to leap like a locust, his majestic snorting, a fright?" (39:19–20). "Is it due to your understanding that the hawk flies, spreading its wings to the south?" (39:26). Most of the other questions are too long to quote here, but they reveal God as the magnificent creator of all things, the One who has all knowledge and power.

Job finally realizes, "I have indeed spoken about things I didn't understand, wonders beyond my comprehension" (Job 42:3). Job repents, and prays also for his friends. At the end of the book, God shows mercy to them all and blesses Job with far more than Job had lost.

From Job's story we learn that as much as we may need people around us to be present and share our grief, sometimes we may need them to be quiet. Instead of offering theological arguments or advice, sometimes they may best share in our suffering by not saying a word. Sometimes we may need to do the talking. That was certainly true for Job as he defended himself to his friends, as he confronted God with his lament, and came to a new understanding of himself and his place in the world.

A number of years before my Dearheart's passing, his job was terminated just before Christmas through no fault of his own and after twenty-five years of solid teaching ministry. As we worked through this painful loss, I researched and wrote a few articles on wrongful job terminations in church and other Christian organizations.[1] As a result, I heard from others with similar experiences. Five, six, ten years or more later, some had never felt free to share their feelings of betrayal and loss. Some had changed churches or denominations, or left ministry altogether. Some had been close to suicide and still struggled with depression and anxiety.

At the same time, some also reported that God surprised them with something even better—time to reflect on their true purpose in life, relocation to a different setting, a renewed sense of trust in God, sometimes even a new and higher paying job. They didn't exactly get over their painful job termination—the old pain would sometimes flare up—but for the most part their grief was no longer a defining event or preoccupation.

From them, I gleaned much wisdom on dealing with loss and grief. Then after my Dearheart died, I revisited those lessons, and they still ring true for me.

Look to those who love you, and hold on to them. Whatever you have lost—whoever you have lost—look to those who remain in your family, friends, church, and community. Look for those who will listen and allow you to grieve in your own way and at your own pace. Know that you are a beloved child of God, of incomparable worth and honor.

Wisdom Along the Way

Work out. Your body was made to move, so don't give in to inertia. Go for a run. Go for a walk. Use a punching bag. Work up a sweat, and work out your anger and other hard feelings.

Allow yourself to vent. Tell your troubles to God. Write out your heartbreak, then burn the pages. Cry. Talk to a friend in confidence.

Assess your situation. What do you need to get by in the short term? When you're ready, consider what you need in the long term in order to thrive. Consult trusted friends who can pray with you. Get professional financial and legal advice as needed, and don't let yourself be rushed into any decisions.

Find things that feed your spirit. Morning coffee on the deck outside. An evening concert. A walk by the ocean. A long bike ride. Fresh cut flowers. A favorite book. Think about your own needs for a change instead of the needs of others. Be gentle with yourself.

Accept offers of help, and look for the good. Cherish every card, every email of support, every word of encouragement. Even if they're far too cheerful for your mood, appreciate the thoughtfulness and know that they're meant well. If you don't have the energy to respond right away, then take a rain check on that invitation to coffee.

Know that there is healing. Have a sense of humor. Get a good night's sleep. Pray. Look for God's open door or window or tunnel into the sunlight. Walk with Jesus, and be guided by the Holy Spirit.

Wisdom Along the Way

HOPE PRACTICE

As a new king, Solomon prayed to God for wisdom, "Please give your servant a discerning mind in order to govern your people and to distinguish good from evil, because no one is able to govern this important people of yours without your help" (1 Kings 3:9). In our new landscape of loss, let us also pray, "Please give us wisdom to order our lives, to discern what is good because we need your help."

If you feel overwhelmed with too much advice and need a time out, feel free to take a break. You don't need to do something just because someone else thinks you should. You can let well-meaning advice go in one ear and out the other, as my father used to say. You can let it pass through without taking any action. That's what I did when someone told me I should get a dog. Or when others said I should go to Europe, or take a cruise, or both. These things might be right for someone else, but I know they're not for me, at least for now.

If you're needing advice, consider what you need and who you might turn to. In my early and middle grief, when I turned to people for advice, it was most often with a practical household

Wisdom Along the Way

question. Like what brand of decaf coffee should I try? Or how do I fix my kitchen faucet handle that's hitting the window sill when it never did that before? To discern the advice I received, I found it helpful to get more than one opinion and compare.

If you're not sure what you need, prayerfully review the lessons in this chapter on looking to those who love you, working out and venting your feelings, discerning what you need to thrive including things that feed your spirit and people who support you. Is God leading you to strengthen one of these areas? What might be the next good step for you?

18

THE COURAGE TO KEEP GOING

Take courage. Ask a favor of Jesus, your light.
ST. TERESA OF AVILA

"How confident are you about _____?" I hadn't been expecting a telephone survey when I answered the phone, and I automatically stopped listening after the first few words. I'm sure the rest of the question went on about *something*, but whatever it was couldn't hold my attention.

My mind was already racing: What kind of question was that? When my Dearheart died, my entire world had shifted, and I no longer felt confident about anything. When people would ask, "How are you?" I wasn't even sure about that. On the world scene, there was—and is—so much uncertainty in so many areas of the world that I wondered how anyone could be confident about anything. Certainly not about the effectiveness of government policy, or the health of the economy, or whatever else was in the rest of that survey.

Hope Beyond Our Sorrows

The year before my Dearheart died, I preached a sermon on 1 John 3:21 (NIV): "Dear friends . . . we have confidence before God." The word *confidence* is the same word for *courage*, and the verse means that we can approach God boldly, with confidence and courage. We don't need to be afraid. We can "reassure our hearts in God's presence," knowing that we belong to God who loves us (3:19). In my grief-fueled crisis of confidence, I clung to that assurance: *Dear friends, we have courage before God.*

In whatever seasons of loss and grief we bear, in our loneliness and distress, whatever is happening in the world around us, whatever is happening in our personal lives—*Dear friends, we have courage before God.*

When you go to church and your grief makes your heart pound so hard that you can hardly hear anything else—*Dear friends, we have courage before God.*

When someone asks, "Why didn't you have a funeral?" and you immediately feel judged even though the question was probably not meant that way—*Dear friends, we have courage before God.*

When you have to keep calling the credit card company about getting a card in your own name because first they send two cards as if you still have a joint account, then they send a new card with the right name but the wrong account number, then the card is approved but never sent, so you're told it's best to reapply, and by then you've been working at the same issue for six weeks, and you've lost all heart—*Dear friends, we have courage before God.*

Again and again, I kept returning to that one sliver of hope. Perhaps I was making too much of it, and applying the words too personally, but that message of reassurance kept me

The Courage to Keep Going

going. Besides, I had lots of company taking courage before God in a personal way. The psalmist faced the threat of enemies and false witnesses by taking courage in God's presence (Psalm 27:11–14). When Peter and John were arrested and put in prison for healing a man crippled from birth, Peter answered the charges boldly by drawing on his courage before God (Acts 4:8–13). Despite the opposition they faced, Paul, Silvanus, and Timothy continued to share the good news of Jesus with "the courage through God" (1 Thessalonians 2:2).

Taking courage doesn't mean that all of our problems will disappear. It doesn't mean that we will sail through every challenge. But it can put the challenges we face in perspective, and renew our energy and sense of purpose. Because we have courage before God, we can persevere through grief, through frustration, through anxiety, through all the challenges of life. Because we have courage before God, we have hope for today and for the future.

This is not courage based on our own inner strength or positive self-talk. Because sometimes we're too weary and weak for any of that. This is not courage based on results. Because sometimes despite our best efforts and most earnest prayers, we don't get our hoped-for results. This is not a courage based on our personal feelings. Because feelings can come and go—depending on whether we had enough sleep last night, depending on whether or not the sun is shining.

At times our own hearts may condemn us with self-doubt, but that hardly matters, because whatever we might think or feel in our hearts, God is greater (1 John 3:20). Our courage before God is grounded in the One who knows us even better than we know ourselves, who loves us so much that Jesus came to lay down his life for us.

Hope Beyond Our Sorrows

So whatever challenges we face in this life, whatever others or our own hearts might say—*Dear friends, we have courage before God.*

I know I'm not the only one to experience a loss of confidence during a season of grief. Sheryl Sandberg had a high-profile job with Facebook and co-authored *Lean In*, a best-selling book on women, work, and leadership. But when her husband died suddenly while they were on vacation with their two children, she, too, experienced a crisis of confidence. She writes:

> For me, my confidence crumbled overnight. It reminded me of watching a house in my neighborhood that had taken years to build get torn down in a matter of minutes. Boom. Flattened.[1]

Others experience a loss of confidence as a result of burnout or the loss of a job. They may lose confidence in their identity and sense of vocation, their skills and experience. They may doubt their sense of judgment, their self-worth, and their ability to find another job. Pastors, missionaries, and other church workers may lose confidence in the church or other sending organization and may even begin to doubt their faith in God. For grievers of all kinds, a loss of confidence may mean second-guessing every decision and even doubting their ability to grieve.

As with other signs and symptoms of grief, a first response might be simply to let those feelings be. It's okay to feel flattened, to feel the loss of the confidence you once had, to not know how to answer a deceptively simple but oh-so-complicated

The Courage to Keep Going

question like *How are you?* Over time, as you get used to grief and feel more able, you might begin to take small steps to rebuild your confidence. Set an achievable goal, and celebrate your progress.

Dear friends, we have courage before God. And if you need some extra help to keep going, take some of that courage to reach out to your pastor, a grief mentor or coach, bereavement counselor, or other helping professional. If you think you're experiencing more complicated grief, please also see chapter 27 of this book.

The Courage to Keep Going

HOPE PRACTICE

Lectio divina is a contemplative practice that helps me slow down and listen to God. A simple version begins with reading a portion of Scripture to get an overall sense of the meaning or story. Then read the same portion a second time, asking God to direct you and noticing where your attention rests. Then read a third time, asking God how the Word applies to your life. I encourage you to try this with Psalm 27:7–14, a psalm that begins in need and ends in courage.

After you've prayerfully read through the passage three times, consider how you will live out what God has shown you. Where do you need courage to keep going?

19

FROM ME TO WE

We bereaved are not alone. We belong to the largest company in all the world—the company of those who have known suffering.

HELEN KELLER, *We Bereaved*

After my Dearheart died, I often felt and acted as if I were the only one grieving—but of course, I was wrong. Although we didn't have children and our parents had passed on years earlier, my Dearheart had brothers. I have sisters. We have other family members, including a niece who would faithfully call every week. They were all stunned at my Dearheart's passing, and our friends and church were too.

I can't say that I was much comfort to any of them, for I was so consumed by grief that I hardly thought about anything or anyone else. If I didn't feel like answering the phone, I didn't answer. If I was invited out to dinner and didn't feel like going, I politely declined and stayed home. In my shock and grief, I could scarcely do more, and I told myself that was all right. I needed to take care of myself. In the short term, perhaps I was right.

But as I look back, I see that the operative word during that time was *I*. The demands of grief had turned me inward,

Hope Beyond Our Sorrows

so *I* focused on how *I* felt, on what *I* needed to get through the day. But I wasn't the only one grieving. I was part of an entire company of people who were grieving the loss of my Dearheart. Then, too, as I thought more broadly of people around the world—people grieving their own personal losses and public tragedies—I realized that Helen Keller was right. Yes, I was part of "the largest company in all the world."[1]

The reality of grieving together is perhaps most obvious and immediate when there are young children involved. When you're the responsible parent, there's no question of moving quickly from me to we in your grief. Love and the realities of daily living shift your focus.

When Trish Hunt's husband was in a serious car accident in another city, she immediately called an aunt to stay with their children while she flew to be with her husband. Family and close friends came to be with them too, and four days later on his twenty-ninth birthday, her husband died from his injuries. She was exhausted and deeply grieving, but she says, "My love for my children and my instinctive desire to protect and provide for them was deeper even than my grief."[2]

When his wife, daughter, and mother were killed in a car accident, Jerry Sittser became a single father to their three other children. As he dealt with his own grief and managed to keep their household going, he writes:

> I have tried to help my children grieve—to make room for their anger, welcome their tears, listen to their complaints, create order out of chaos, and do this work of comfort in

a way that is sensitive to timing and to the unique personality of each child.[3]

In her book *Breathing Through Grief*, Dorina Lazo Gilmore-Young offers some guidance on helping children grieve. When her husband died, their daughters were just two, five, and eight years old. In the decade since then, she's learned a lot and recommends being direct with your children and keeping communication open. Share your tears, and allow them to do the same. Be creative and engage them in the process. As one example, she says, "Each year I invite them to help me think of creative ways to honor their dad on anniversaries and holidays."[4]

The early church was encouraged to "mourn with those who mourn" (Romans 12:15 NIV), and Scripture offers numerous examples of mourning as a shared practice. Job's three friends came to sit with him, they wept together, and tore their clothes as a sign of mourning (Job 2:11–13). When King Saul and his son Jonathan were killed, and the rest of their army scattered or dead on the battlefield, David and his soldiers also tore their clothes and mourned with tears and fasting. David sang a funeral song, and ordered everyone in Judah to learn it (2 Samuel 1:1–27). Jesus cried with Mary and the others who mourned over the death of Lazarus (John 11:33–36).

In our own day, we might not tear our clothes, but we mourn with those who mourn in other ways. Funerals, memorial services, and celebrations of life give opportunity for family and friends to share memories, music, prayers, hugs, words

Hope Beyond Our Sorrows

of Scripture, food, tears, and even laughter. More informal gatherings in homes or outdoors can serve the same purpose. During the pandemic, in lieu of a large gathering, I appreciated receiving and responding to the many cards from family, friends, and even distant acquaintances. Some grieve together in support groups. Others, like Dorina Lazo Gilmore-Young and her daughters, may do something special as a family on the anniversary of a death.

As a pastor walking alongside people who were grieving, I had sometimes recommended a group or a counselor for additional support beyond family, friends, and church. Some had found support groups helpful. Others had not. Some tried a few different counselors before finding one that seemed a good fit. As with anything else, no group or counselor is "one size fits all."

In lieu of any kind of formal group, I met regularly with a friend who had been widowed a number of years earlier. One of my Dearheart's best friends who was also a pastor would check in with me often. "I am always here for phone calls, emails, texts, whatever you need from me," he said. "I will keep in touch; I am in this for the long haul." And he was.

From Me to We

HOPE PRACTICE

Consider the me and we of your grief. In what ways do you need to take care of yourself at this stage in your grief? Make a list, and be specific. If you need to move around more, choose a specific activity and write it down. Like take a twenty-minute walk, or bike once around the park, or some other measurable and doable goal. If you need to get more rest, you might write "go to bed before midnight." Then decide when you will do these things, and enter them in your calendar or datebook.

Who are the "we" who share your grief? In what ways have you been able to grieve together? Are there some things you still need to do? If you have children living at home, consider the recommendations from Dorina Lazo Gilmore-Young. How might you be creative and keep the lines of communication open? What practices would you add?

O God of all consolation, we pray for all those who are grieving in our own circles and around the world. Provide for those who are thirsty and hungry. Protect those oppressed by injustice and by circumstances beyond their control. Comfort the lonely and grieving. Care for those in need. Renew our hope in you.

20

SORROWFUL, YET REJOICING

But unless we make space for grief, we cannot know the depths of the love of God, the healing God wrings from pain, the way grieving yields wisdom, comfort, even joy.
TISH HARRISON WARREN, *Prayer in the Night*

In a corner of my garden near the front door, the figure of an angel reads a book. She's well-weathered by the seasons, but I love to see her there, always reading in the rain or snow or sun, absorbed in her book whatever the weather might be. She reminds me that even in our digital world, there are still avid readers. She reminds me, too, of the passage of time, and of my friends Tom and Maria, who gave her to me years ago after I led the funeral services for their son.

At the age of twenty-one, Derek was athletic and fun-loving, with a contagious enthusiasm for life. His family and friends said he could turn an ordinary day into an adventure. But one night, Derek was struck and killed by a car, and his life abruptly cut short. His ordinary days and adventures on this earth were over. Suddenly we were all in mourning for the vibrant young man he had been and the man he would have become.

Months later with Christmas coming, Maria started to write Christmas cards as usual. Derek had loved Christmas and was always the first in the family to get out the decorations. But clearly, life without Derek was no longer life as usual, and that Christmas was no longer Christmas as usual. For all the joy of the season, for all the joy of celebrating the birth of Jesus, his mother wondered how she could wish anyone a *Merry Christmas* when her heart still ached with sorrow.

That's when she came up with the idea of *sorjoy*—a unique word to express both her sorrow and joy. It was an apt description of her feelings that Christmas, and since then it's stuck with me too. My first Christmas without my Dearheart? *Sorjoy.* Celebrating the first wedding on his side of the family without him? *Sorjoy.* Cooking his favorite dish of chicken stir-fried with fresh lemon and slivers of ginger? *Sorjoy.*

I hadn't planned to go to my high school reunion. My Dearheart and I had gone to the same high school in the same grade. We both had school friends, and had kept in touch with a few over the years, but for the most part, those old friendships were in the past. We had moved out of the city, to the United States for a few years, and then to the Fraser Valley. Life had moved on for all of us, and we hadn't looked back. My Dearheart and I had never gone to any of the reunions.

But this year was special—our fiftieth high school reunion! The planning committee had gone all out. They set up a private Facebook group to prepare for the celebration. They searched for lost classmates. They planned swag bags, gathered photos

Sorrowful, Yet Rejoicing

to project on screen, chose music. They reserved a room at a private golf club and arranged for a fancy buffet.

"Are you going to the reunion?" a friend asked as we chatted before our writers group meeting. He had been one of the valedictorians for our graduating class from high school, and now lived in the Valley too.

I shook my head. "I've never gone to any of the reunions. And now, I don't think I'd want to go alone."

Later that day, he sent me an email. His wife had suggested that they invite me to go to the reunion with them. They would pick me up and bring me home, door-to-door service for the long drive there and back. "We would love to have you join us."

What a kind and thoughtful invitation! How could I say no? Yet how could I say yes? Just thinking about the reunion made my heart beat faster. Like the first Christmas without my Dearheart, my first high school reunion without him would definitely be *sorjoy*.

But of course, I accepted their invitation—and I enjoyed the reunion more than I thought I would. Visiting with my friends on the drive there and back helped calm me down. I loved the floral centrepieces on each table, the balloons for the photo corner, and the elegant buffet with a wide selection of appetizers. It felt good to connect with former classmates who had come from across the country and out of the country. Some had heard of my Dearheart's passing and offered their condolences. Others hadn't heard and innocently asked how he was, but I got through those awkward moments. Later as I was leaving, another friend pulled me aside and said, "I looked across the room and saw you laughing, so I knew you were okay."

I didn't know how to tell her that for me, the reunion had been all *sorjoy*. But yes, I was okay.

In the book of Ruth, when Naomi held her grandson, I imagine that was a *sorjoy* moment for her. She had lived through the death of her husband and two sons. She had wondered how she might survive without them. But now her grief was attended by joy as well. Now she had a new family, a grandson who would be like a son to her.

Sorrow and joy appear together throughout the Bible. The psalmist writes, "Weeping may stay all night, but by morning, joy!" (Psalm 30:5). "You changed my mourning into dancing. You took off my funeral clothes and dressed me up in joy" (Psalm 30:11). To prepare his disciples for his death and resurrection, Jesus says to them, "You have sorrow now; but I will see you again, and you will be overjoyed. No one takes away your joy" (John 16:22). As servants of God facing many afflictions as they spread the good news of Jesus, the apostle Paul describes himself and Timothy as "sorrowful, yet always rejoicing" (2 Corinthians 6:10 NIV).

Sorrow and joy might seem like contradictions, but I've been to many funerals with *sorjoy* moments, with families in tears over missing their loved one, then laughing at a funny story. Or smiling at a favorite picture that also makes them cry. Or feeling sad that their loved one is gone, yet happy that family

Sorrowful, Yet Rejoicing

and friends have gathered together to remember. In *sorjoy* moments, tears—and laughter—can be healthy and healing.

Those who are grieving may feel especially vulnerable at Christmas and other special times of the year. So give yourself an extra measure of grace. Remember that it's all right to feel happy, sad, or both at the same time. If *Merry Christmas* seems too jolly, you could switch to *Have a blessed Christmas* or *Praying for peace this Christmas*. You might even skip sending Christmas cards entirely.

Sometimes it can be helpful to prepare for *sorjoy* moments. Before going to my high school reunion, I asked the organizers if they were planning any kind of memorial. Some reunions create a special display to remember classmates who have died. Others might have a roll call or an empty chair to represent those who have gone on before. But to my relief, our committee decided instead simply to focus on those who would be present at the reunion. I'm glad I asked so that I would know what—and what not—to expect.

Sorrowful, Yet Rejoicing

HOPE PRACTICE

How have sorrow and joy been part of your grieving?

Are there some times ahead when you might feel especially vulnerable? Like the anniversary of your loss. Thanksgiving or Christmas. Your loved one's birthday. Other special days. What might you do to prepare?

Sorjoy moments can come at any time, when we're least prepared. Ready or not, let those moments come.

O God of our sorrow, God of our joy—you are God with us in every moment. O Jesus who wept at the grave of Lazarus—Jesus, who joyfully called him to life—by your Spirit, lift the weight of our sorrow and grant us your light.

PART THREE

Present Grief
A Way Forward

21

REMEMBER THE WONDERS

Pursue the LORD and his strength; seek his face always!
Remember the wondrous works he has done.
PSALM 105:4–5

Psalm 105 is a story-telling psalm that traces the journey of the Israelite community: from God's call to Abraham, to their slavery in Egypt, to their journey through the desert, to their new life in the promised land. It's a story of God's goodness, protection, and provision. It's a story filled with thanks and praise.

But that's not the way the same story is told in Exodus 16. In Exodus 16, the people were in the desert on their way to the Promised Land. So they were on the same journey described in Psalm 105. But in Exodus 16, the story does not center on thanks and praise to God; instead, the story is one of great complaint:

In the desert the whole community grumbled against Moses and Aaron. The Israelites said to them, "If only we had died by the LORD's hand in Egypt! There we sat around pots of meat and ate all the food we wanted, but you have

brought us out into this desert to starve this entire assembly to death.
—Exodus 16:2–3 (NIV)

Really? No question that the people's journey through the desert was difficult. Water was scarce, and some of the water that the people had found was too bitter to drink. They were hot and tired and thirsty. But Egypt was not as wonderful as they reimagined it. They had been slaves. No leisurely sitting by the pots cooking meat and eating as much bread as they wanted. No day of rest. No other days off. No weekends. No statutory holidays. No vacation. Just unrelenting work making bricks or doing hard labor out in the fields. God had delivered them from that slavery!

What's more, the people didn't starve in the desert. Instead, God provided them with bread and quails to eat as much as they needed. That was the wonder of it all—and that's what Psalm 105 celebrates. The psalmist remembers the wonders, remembers all the miraculous things that God had done to bring the people out of slavery, remembers how God miraculously provided for the people's needs in the desert.

Like the Israelites in Exodus 16, I might look at my journey of grief and complain—and sometimes I do. How could my Dearheart be taken from me just when he seemed to be getting better? How can I manage without him? I can't manage without my life partner and soul mate.

But like Psalm 105, I can also look back and remember the wonders. How God brought my Dearheart through his first cancer. How even when the cancer recurred, my Dearheart received excellent medical care. Despite the rigors of chemotherapy, he could say, "Sometimes I forget that I'm sick." Although he had taken a leave from teaching, he was well enough to continue working a few hours a day at home, and created a set of animated videos to teach New Testament Greek. That was one of his passions, and even after he died, some students continued to use his videos for self-study, so they could learn to read the New Testament in the original Greek language. Those were all "wonders that God has done"!

During the time of his illness, our church surrounded us in prayer, faithfully praying for my Dearheart every week—and even more often, whenever we had a special prayer request. Our family and friends loved and supported us through that time, and love and support me even now. Those are all wonders that God has done!

Two years after my Dearheart died, one of his former students contacted me, and said that he had taken many of his courses. He said, "Your husband has been so inspirational for me. I am being ordained this year, and would like to invite you to come on his behalf." How touching to receive this note from one of my Dearheart's former students that I had never met. Of course, I gladly attended his ordination, another *sor-joy* moment and another wonder!

Maybe you have good reason to complain. Maybe you've lost a loved one too soon. Or lost a long-standing friendship. Maybe you're dealing with personal health challenges. With concerns

Hope Beyond Our Sorrows

for your kids or aging parents or other family members. With relationship challenges or challenges in your church. With work stress around budget issues, or having enough staff, or other pressures. Or maybe your circle of grief is even wider—including others who have lost their homes and belongings to hurricane or wildfire or flooding or other climate disasters, the ongoing war in Ukraine, the suffering in Gaza, and so many other situations in the world that might not make the headlines, but where there is great loss and suffering.

For these and other significant losses, you might well be asking: Why did God allow that to happen? Why, God? How long, O Lord? Rain down your compassion. Rain down your mercy. And bring relief to me and to others.

There's no complaining in Psalm 105. But in the same story as told in Exodus 16, the people were under such distress that the whole congregation complained. There's plenty of complaining throughout the book of Psalms. Some scholars say that about 40 percent of the psalms are lament—which includes complaining and other expressions of grief or suffering.

Psalm 5:1: "Hear my words, LORD. Consider my groans!" Psalm 13:1: "How long will you forget me, LORD? Forever?" Or Psalm 22:1 that Jesus quotes on the cross: "My God! My God, why have you left me all alone?"

When we complain, when we lament the way things are, we have a lot of company in the psalms. Lament and complaining are not all bad. We might say they're even necessary—in Exodus 16, in the witness of the Psalms, and in our own lives. Lament acknowledges the reality of suffering and the complexity of life. Lament is an act of protest, an act of prayer that leads to praise.[1] Lament and complaining are not the last word.

Remember the Wonders

So while Psalm 5 begins with lament, it ends with words of blessing. While Psalm 13 pointedly asks, "How long?" it ends with a testimony to God's goodness. While Psalm 22 cries out "Why have you left me all alone?" it also praises God for listening. So, too, the complaints of Exodus 16 give way to praise in Psalm 105, perhaps with the wisdom of hindsight developed over the years. In the psalms, in the story of the Israelite community—and I hope for us too—lament leads to praise.

Whatever losses we have endured, however our journey of grief continues today, when we find ourselves complaining, we can bring our lament to God. Surely, God will hear us. God will provide and care for us. Then by God's strength and by God's grace, may we also remember the wonders that God has done. Then may our lament give way to praise and thanksgiving.

Remember the Wonders

HOPE PRACTICE

If you need to lament before you remember God's wonders, take some time to list your complaints and questions before God. You may find it helpful to write these down, but don't hold on to them. Crumple them in a ball and throw them into your recycling bin. Or shred them into tiny pieces and then recycle them or use them as mulch in your garden. Then when you are ready, turn to consider God's wonders.

To remember God's wonders, I've found it helpful to keep a gratitude list. Not a general list that might apply to anyone, like I'm thankful for my family, or I'm thankful for food. But a list of more specific things unique to my life and that change from day to day. Like I'm thankful that my sister arrived safely from Alberta to visit me. Or I'm thankful that I tried a new recipe for rice with pork and Thai basil, and it's now one of my favorite comfort foods.

For a time, I wrote out three specific things every evening, with no repeats. For me it was a form of prayer, a beautiful soul care practice that allowed me to take a moment to remember God's wonders, to give thanks, and to rest in gratitude at the end of the day.

Remember the Wonders

Remember God's wonders in your own life by reviewing your day. Where have you seen God at work? What has lifted your spirits and brought joy to your life? How has God helped you in your daily activities? Write them down. Be specific. Be personal. Give thanks to God!

22

A LOVELY
REMEMBRANCE

Death ends a life, not a relationship.
MITCH ALBOM, *Tuesdays With Morrie*

I want to do all I can to get stronger and come home and be with you forever or for as long as I can," my Dearheart said to me.

By that time, he had been in the hospital for three weeks, dealing with one complication after another related to his cancer. But finally, each complication had been addressed. Finally, he was feeling better. Finally, it seemed he would soon be strong enough to come home.

"I want that too," I said. "But if anything becomes too hard or too painful—the medical system, the treatments, life itself—you can also go." I don't know why I said that since he was clearly recovering.

And I don't know why I thought next about how he had been watching the Olympics when I arrived at the hospital that morning. When I had asked him, "Do you want to keep watching?" he had said, "No, I'd rather talk to you."

With that in mind, I added more as a joke than anything else, "But if you go, I'll still be talking to you."

"Yeah, people will look in and see you talking to an empty hospital bed," he said with a smile.

"No, I'll do that at home," I said, smiling back at him.

Days later I wondered, did he somehow know even then that soon his hospital bed would be empty, but he would not be coming home with me? Did I know at some level even then that I would be at home alone without him? Had we somehow been subconsciously preparing ourselves for the grief to come? For later that evening, there was yet one more complication, and instead of bringing him safely home to me, God brought my Dearheart safely to our eternal home.

I talked with my friend Betty about this. Betty has been one of my closest friends since we were both in high school. I still remember the day she told me she had met the most wonderful man. She and her husband, Erwin, had their wedding just two weeks before my Dearheart and I were married. For years, the four of us were part of an international supper group with friends, hosting, preparing, and eating the most fabulous potlucks featuring food from Ireland, Italy, Greece, Morocco, Korea, Australia, and many other countries. When Betty and Erwin celebrated their twenty-fifth wedding anniversary, my Dearheart was their emcee.

One day Betty and I were having another one of our hour-long phone calls. As we said goodbye, I said, "Say hi to Erwin for me," and she replied, "Say hi to Gary for me." She had said those same words to me many times before, but now with my Dearheart gone, I wasn't sure what to make of them. When she said them again at the end of our next phone

A Lovely Remembrance

call, I said, "I know you remember about my talking to Gary, about how he always wanted to talk to me. But I don't know how I feel about your saying that. It seems so awkward to me now."

"For me, it's a lovely remembrance," she said.

At that, the awkwardness fell away, and now whenever she says, "Say hi to Gary for me," I think of it as a lovely remembrance too.

When I listen to music as I'm cooking or doing some other household chore, I might hear a particular song and spontaneously say, "Oh this was always one of your favorites." (My Dearheart had a lot of favorites.) Or out in the garden, enjoying the sun and fresh air and admiring my roses, I might think, "You knew I would need a garden." (He knew I needed a reason to get outside every day.)

Not long ago I heard the news that the Right Honorable Beverly McLachlin had decided to retire from her role as a foreign judge on Hong Kong's Court of Final Appeal. She had been one of my Dearheart's law school professors, and he had continued to follow her career from professor to judge to supreme court to chief justice of Canada to international jurist. "Who else but you would appreciate this news?" I wondered. "Who can I tell?" And I heard him—imagined him?—saying with a smile, "You can always tell me."

At one time, this kind of inner dialogue was judged to be a sign of unresolved grief, something that got in the way of real relationships with real, living people. But in *The Grieving Brain*, psychology professor and researcher Dr. Mary-Frances

O'Connor says, "More recent research has shown that although wide variation exists in these inner relationships, many people adjust well by maintaining a connection to the deceased."[1]

My friend Vi and her husband would often spend their Saturday mornings on various household chores. When it was time to take a break, he would make and pour their coffee, stir in his cream, and tap his spoon against his coffee cup: clink, clink, clink. Now years after his passing, in memory of her husband, Vi still sometimes taps her spoon on her coffee cup and says, "Good morning, Sweetie. Love ya, Mike!"

Another woman remembers her husband every morning when she has her devotions and lights a candle with her husband's picture on it. She loves hearing their children and grandchildren share their memories of him. At their first family gathering without him, they set a plate for him at the table. One of my Facebook friends lost his wife a number of years ago, yet he still posts on her Facebook page to remember her birthday, to share family photos, her favorite hymn, and other memories.

A daughter remembers her mother by baking her mom's secret recipe chocolate chip cookies. A grandson wears his grandpa's shirt. Some bereaved parents remember their child's birthday every year with a family gathering, or volunteering their time in the community, or making a donation to charity.

These are just a few examples of healthy connections that continue even after an earthly life has ended. The person has

A Lovely Remembrance

died, but the relationship hasn't. Such lovely remembrances bring comfort and even humor in the midst of loss—not by denying the reality of loss, not as a substitute for real relationships in this life, but to honor our loved ones and the relationships that were and are so precious.

A Lovely Remembrance

HOPE PRACTICE

Canadian storyteller Stuart McLean tells the tender and gently humorous story of Art and Betty Gillespie, who lived in the fictional town of Big Narrows on Cape Breton Island in Nova Scotia. When Art was terminally ill with cancer, they traveled all the way to Florida for one last special vacation. Betty had to pay for four seats, so Art could lie down on the flight there and back. But as Betty said, "I figured out that there were no emergencies anymore. We were beyond emergencies, so we might as well travel."

Art and Betty would read to one another in the evenings, and on the night he passed away, they were partway through a book of short stories. After Art's funeral, when Betty couldn't sleep, she took the book, a flashlight, and a lawn chair to his graveside and read the book to him. She did that every night for a week and a half until the book was finished.[2]

What lovely remembrance do you have of people you have loved and lost?

God of comfort, may our good memories outweigh the painful ones, may our tears be tempered by laughter. May we know your love that never fails.

23

EVERY LIFE LEAVES A LEGACY

What you leave behind is not what is engraved in stone monuments, but what is woven into the lives of others.
PERICLES

Let me show you what I learned from our friend Annalee," said Lydia.

My Dearheart and I had recently moved from our house into the townhouse complex where Lydia lived, and she had stopped to chat when she saw me in the front yard near our two new-to-us rhododendron bushes. I loved the showy red blossoms that brightened the walkway to our front door. But the magnificent display was over—the flowers had faded, turned limp, and now clung sadly to the leaves. I'd never had rhodos before, so I wasn't sure how best to care for them.

"When the flowers are finished, you can remove them like this," Lydia said. With one hand, she steadied a branch, and with the other she carefully pinched the base of a spent blossom, gave it a twist, and removed it without disturbing the new growth underneath. It was quick and easy and required no special tools. A perfect project for an amateur gardener like me. So I followed Lydia's example and took my time patiently removing all of the spent blossoms.

I've done that every summer since, and during that quiet time, I remember Annalee. She had passed away in hospice the year before Lydia showed me how to deadhead my rhododendrons. I had led her graveside and funeral services, and Lydia had given a beautiful tribute to our friend. Annalee had enjoyed her kids and grandkids, music and travel, getting together with her Bible study group, and volunteering in the church and wider community. But she had also experienced loss. The death of her parents. The death of her husband, Jake. The loss of her health when she was diagnosed with cancer. Yet even when she became so ill and weak, I remember Annalee calmly saying to me, "It's not a bad life. I have time to read, to look out my window, and listen to music. I have time to pray."

To the end of her life, Annalee's deep desire was to be a faithful witness to Jesus, and her desire was fulfilled. She left behind a beautiful legacy of faith and service. She left behind many good memories for her family, friends, and church. And even though she never knew it, she even left me a small legacy in how best to care for my rhododendrons. She had passed on her love and knowledge of gardening to Lydia, who passed them on to me.

When we think of leaving a legacy, we might think first of leaving money or property. At least, that's one dictionary definition of a legacy. So we might hear of a large bequest when someone donates a new hospital wing or builds a new library for a university. Leaving a legacy might mean setting

Every Life Leaves a Legacy

up a college scholarship or donating an old homestead to a museum.

But a legacy is more than such large-scale social projects. Every life leaves a legacy—a lasting impact made of a lifetime of simple everyday actions. One man is remembered as a caring listener who always appreciated a good story. He delighted in his family and friends, his wider circle of relatives and church family. He enjoyed fishing, woodworking, and laughing with his grandchildren. All that—and more—is part of his legacy.

At the age of twenty-one, when Derek was struck by a car and tragically killed one night, his life was over far too soon, yet he also left a legacy. His family, friends, and teammates on his hockey team all spoke of his passion for life, how his exuberance was contagious, and his fun-loving nature would often lift their spirits. One night after a big game, when he was asked for his winning stick, Derek impulsively climbed onto the boards surrounding the rink and just as impulsively handed his stick over the plexiglass to his young fan. His fun-loving, generous spirit is part of his legacy.

Yet not every legacy is a happy one. Sometimes a death leaves a painful legacy of bad memories, hard feelings, and unfinished business.

After the death of acclaimed Canadian novelist Alice Munro, her daughter, Andrea Skinner, published an essay about the sexual abuse she had experienced from her stepfather. At nine years old, Skinner had been living with her father and stepmother, but while on a visit to her mother and stepfather, he began abusing her. Skinner was in her twenties

Hope Beyond Our Sorrows

when she finally wrote a letter to her mother telling her about the abuse, but Alice Munro stayed with her husband. Years later, he was charged and convicted of sexual assault, yet still she stayed with him.

Mother and daughter never reconciled. And now that the abuse has been made public, many ask, with all of Munro's insight into human relationships in her books, how could she have stayed? What does this mean for how we are to read and understand her novels? She left behind a legacy of great writing, but she also left a great legacy of pain for her daughter.

When my Dearheart's job was terminated after twenty-five years of faithful and effective service as a college professor, he was stunned. Suddenly the college was no longer his family as he had always been led to believe. Suddenly he was cut off and left with a legacy of painful questions. Why was he told his termination was for financial reasons, but asked to say he was retiring? Why was he asked to sign a nondisclosure agreement? He refused to sign, and refused to say he was retiring. In fact, he went on to teach graduate students elsewhere. But the success that followed never fully made up for the painful legacy he had received from his previous employer.

Every Life Leaves a Legacy

HOPE PRACTICE

Every life leaves a legacy. Every loss leaves a legacy, for good or ill. For those of us left behind to pick up the shattered pieces of our lives, the legacy that is left to us might shape or misshape us, might grow us in faith and trust in God, or make us more wary of trusting anyone.

Consider the legacy you have received. Give thanks for all that is positive. Grieve over those things that are difficult. Know that you are not alone, and that this is not the end of your story. My Dearheart coped with the painful legacy he received by journaling, talking with a trusted friend, refusing to dwell on the ANTs (automatic negative thoughts),[1] and replacing them with more positive thoughts. These things did not come easily to him, but they were a reminder that he was not the painful legacy he had received. You are not the painful legacy you have received.

God, we give you thanks for all your goodness, for your promises of faith, hope, and love. Where we have been left with painful experiences and unresolved issues, where our memories bring unrest instead of comfort, help us to release these things to you. Grant us healing and peace. Lord, have mercy. Christ, have mercy.

24

ON NOT GETTING
OVER GRIEF

Our goal shifts from escaping the clutches of grief to living a worthwhile life with grief as a companion we don't mind.

ANNA DARBONNE, *Navigating Grief Workbook*

Before the COVID-19 pandemic—when paying with cash was more common than it is today—my Dearheart would pay with a bill, pocket the change, then come home and add the coins to a small plastic tub that he kept in the corner of the bedroom closet. The nickels, dimes, quarters, dollar and two-dollar coins added up, and every so often he would sort, count, and roll them into neat bundles and donate them to charity for relief and development. This was his way of setting aside money for an extra donation on top of our regular giving, a way to remember the needs of others around the world even as he went about his daily activities. Besides, my Dearheart didn't like the weight of coins in his pockets.

But then the pandemic happened. Paying cash was out, and the tub of coins sat unused in the corner of the closet. Then my Dearheart was diagnosed with a recurrence of cancer. Then he

Hope Beyond Our Sorrows

was gone. He never got the chance to donate the last rolls of coins as he had planned.

Finally, two years after my Dearheart's death, I thought I should do something about that tub of coins. I thought I could deposit the coins at the credit union, then write a check for relief and development as my Dearheart had wanted to do. But when I looked in the tub, I discovered that he had not only rolled up all of the loose coins, but he had labeled several of the rolls *U.S.*

With both Canadian and US currencies, suddenly it seemed too awkward to deposit them at the credit union and write a check. Instead, I emailed the local office of my Dearheart's chosen charity to ask if they would accept the coins as is. It seemed my question was rather unusual, since the person who received it needed to check first with the finance department. But I soon received a reply: yes, I could donate the rolls of coins by bringing them to the office.

So the next week, I transferred the rolls of coins to a small cardboard box, dropped it off at the office, and continued with several other errands. I suppose I should have felt good about all of that. The overall dollar amount wasn't much, but I had honored my Dearheart's wishes. I had cleaned up a corner of the bedroom closet. Finished another chore. Crossed another thing off the list, as some might say.

But I didn't feel good about it at all. I felt horrible. I felt unhappy and anxious and stressed out—for no good reason at all, and yet for every reason. What was a box of coins in the face of the crises in Gaza, Ukraine, southern Sudan, and many other places around the world? What good would it do for those in need of food, shelter, and other supplies? And what was I to do with my Dearheart gone? I was sick of death and grief in my own heart and in the world at large.

On Not Getting Over Grief

One thing I keep learning and relearning is that healing from grief is a process that tends to circle back on itself even as it moves forward. As C. S. Lewis wrote about his own grief over the death of his wife:

> In grief, nothing "stays put." One keeps on emerging from a phase, but it always recurs. Round and round. Everything repeats. Am I going in circles, or dare I hope I am on a spiral?
>
> But if a spiral, am I going up or down it?[1]

It doesn't take much to send me down the spiral. Donating my Dearheart's stash of coins. Learning that one of my former classmates had a stroke and passed away not long after I had talked with him at our high school reunion. The death of a good friend that same summer. A celebration of life that I led for a young man who had died of a drug overdose. One of the slides during the service had shown him at home as a child with his older sister, with my Dearheart and me beside them. Seeing it added another layer of emotion to an already emotional service. But in a way it seemed like a tribute to my Dearheart too, how we were such partners in life and ministry. As each death, each loss recalls another, down the spiral I go under their weight until I start moving up again.

Will this spiral ever end?

International grief experts Elisabeth Kubler-Ross and David Kessler write:

The reality is that you will grieve forever. You will not "get over" the loss of a loved one; you will learn to live with it. You will heal and you will rebuild yourself around the loss you have suffered. You will be whole again but you will never be the same. Nor should you be the same nor would you want to.[2]

Their wisdom is borne out by the experience of others.

Months after my Dearheart died, ninety-one-year-old actor, producer, and screenwriter William Shatner celebrated the release of his latest book, *Boldly Go: Reflections on a Life of Awe and Wonder*. He was asked by a morning show host if he would mind talking about the death of his wife, Nerine. She had died by drowning over twenty years earlier, but Shatner's voice trembled when he answered. The host asked, "It never goes away, does it?"

Shatner replied, "It doesn't. Grief is a palpable entity in the human experience. Grief has sides to it. Depending on how you deal with it, it can be assuaged. But it never goes away."[3]

For another example of learning to live with grief, I look to my friends Bev and Clare. Ten years ago, their oldest son was diagnosed with lymphoma and showed incredible courage and grace through eighteen months of treatment. Russ and his wife had two children who shared his love of learning and music. He worked as an IT director at a Christian college, and had many interests, including hockey, motorcycles, and reading. For his fortieth birthday, he asked that people spread love, for "it is the only thing in this life that endures." A few days

On Not Getting Over Grief

later, he sent a message to his friends that his treatment plan was changing to comfort care, and a few days after that he was gone.

As parents, Bev and Clare deeply mourned the loss of their son, and even now a fresh burst of grief can surprise them at any moment. Hearing someone else's story of grief, receiving an emotional insight, being in a particular place, even hearing a sound or noticing a certain smell can move one or both of them to silent tears or renewed sobbing.

Clare says, "We may not feel as handicapped emotionally as we once did, and we do not expect, nor wish to be free from these experiences. They are now part of our story, and in some ways that of millions who have come and gone in the larger human story. We feel that we are at peace, and have an unwavering sense of trust in God's grace and loving kindness, which Russ also declared before he died." In some ways, grief is still their companion, but over time and by God's grace, they have learned to live through it and with it.

On Not Getting Over Grief

HOPE PRACTICE

On the day I donated my Dearheart's coins, the sudden wave of grief took me by surprise. I didn't feel like continuing with the rest of my errands, so I sat for a few moments in the car, practiced a few calming breaths, offered a prayer, and sat in silence some more. Then I decided to carry on as I had planned, stopping for groceries at the Asian market on my way home. But instead of heating up leftovers for lunch, I made a new plan for a self-care treat: to pick up take-out, give myself the afternoon off, and call a friend.

The prophet Isaiah proclaims the word of the Lord:

> Don't fear, for I have redeemed you;
> I have called you by name; you are mine.
> When you pass through the waters, I will be with you;
> when through the rivers, they won't sweep over you.
> When you walk through the fire, you won't be scorched
> and flame won't burn you.
> —Isaiah 43:1–2

When we pass through new waves of grief, God will be with us. When through rivers of grief, they won't sweep over us. When

On Not Getting Over Grief

grief burns like fire, we won't be scorched and the flame won't burn us. We don't need to be afraid, for God has redeemed us and called us by name.

When have you experienced an unexpected burst of grief? What helped you get through it? Give thanks for God's presence and protection.

25

THROUGH GRIEF TO GIVING

For it is in giving that we receive.
ST. FRANCIS OF ASSISI

Last summer I reconnected with a friend at our high school reunion, and several months later we decided to have a longer visit. I would come into the city to join her church for Sunday morning worship, then we would have lunch together after the service. I looked forward to seeing her, and I was also curious about the church, for at one time it had been my church—our church. My Dearheart and I had been part of the youth and young adult groups, he was baptized in that church, and we had been married there. Although we later moved away and hadn't been part of the congregation for years, the church held many warm memories for me.

The sanctuary looked the same as I remembered it, with the red carpet, wooden pews, and stained glass windows along each side. But there was a screen at the front now, and the wooden pulpit had been replaced by a clear podium. The scripture reading that morning was from the gospel of Mark, the story of the poor widow who came to the temple and put two coins in the offering box, a familiar story to me that I've read many times, that I've studied and preached and written about. Yet that morning, it struck me in a new and more personal way.

A pastor led the prayer that followed the scripture reading, and made reference to the widow who had offered her two coins, everything she had to live on. In his prayer, he identified with the story so strongly, imagining himself in her place, that he confessed, "I'm not sure I'm there yet."

As he identified with her story, I did too, and the thought suddenly struck me: *I am the poor widow. What do I have to give?* I hardly heard the rest of the prayer as the thought came to me with such force: *I am the poor widow.* That might seem obvious to you and anyone else, but although my Dearheart died over two years ago, I never think of myself as a widow. The word seems foreign and old-fashioned to me. Besides, I still think of myself as married. I still feel married. I still wear my wedding ring. On financial and government documents, I only reluctantly check the box that says *widow.* I know that's the proper legal definition, but that's not the way I feel.

I don't like being pigeonholed in a box that says *widow.* And maybe you resist whatever pigeonhole other people or institutions have for you too. Single/Married/Divorced/Widowed. Employed/Unemployed/Student/Retired. Youth/Young Adult/Middle-Aged/Senior. Such broad categories can be useful in determining trends and planning for the present and future, in establishing congregational ministries and social programs, eligibility for funding, and responding in other ways as a church and wider community. More personally, we can use them to

Through Grief to Giving

reflect on our own situations, assess our needs, and help us move forward in practical ways. But those broad categories tell only a partial story. They are not the entire definition of who we are.

In Mark's story of the woman who comes to the temple with her offering, we are told that she is a poor widow. Knowing something of her social location helps us understand some of the challenges she faced. In the time of Jesus, there were many poor widows, with few options to support themselves, dependent on their grown sons or other family members, or gleaning in the fields for food as Ruth had done generations earlier. When faced with injustice, they often had no one to plead their case for them (Luke 18:1–5). Just a few verses before the story of the poor widow and her offering, Jesus criticizes legal experts "who cheat widows out of their homes" (Mark 12:40). Such was the widow's lot: often poor in material things, poor in opportunities to support herself, vulnerable to abuse and fraud, dependent on her family or the church.

When the woman in Mark's story came to the temple grounds, others may have ignored or dismissed her as just one more poor widow in Jerusalem. But Jesus saw her. He truly saw her for who she was—beyond the loss of her husband, beyond her social location, beyond whatever pigeonholes others might have for her. In fact, Jesus was so excited by her example of faith that he called his disciples together for a teachable moment.

He said to them, "This poor widow has put in more than everyone who's been putting money in the treasury" (Mark 12:43). Jesus had been watching—which wasn't as rude then as it might seem to us today. The trumpet-shaped offering boxes were lined up in the Court of Women so everyone could see. Some people wanted to be seen as they made their offerings (Matthew 6:2). But they had no reason to be proud, for as Jesus noted, the woman's two coins amounted to more than all the other offerings. Others had given what they could spare, but the woman had given everything she had to live on (Mark 12:44).

We don't know when the woman's husband died, whether she had young children at home, or adult children who supported her. Did she spend long days gleaning in the fields just to have enough to eat and perhaps trade for the other necessities of life? What was her grief journey, and how was she grieving still?

We're not privy to any of that, but we see her faith in action. As a woman, she could only go so far in the temple, as far as the Court of Women. The inner courts were off limits to her, but still she went to the temple and entered as far as she could. She got as close to God as she could. She held on to faith, despite her loss, despite her poverty, despite the social and religious limitations of her time and culture.

She gave sacrificially, not thinking of herself and her own needs, but giving as she had determined and as she had felt able to give. If anyone else had been watching, they might have said she gave more than she was able to give. They might well have said she gave foolishly. Certainly she wasn't acting like an impoverished widow. She had stepped beyond the pigeonhole that others had for her. She was clearly able to look beyond herself to God, to look beyond herself to offering what she could for the sake of others.

I am the poor widow. What do I have to give?

Through Grief to Giving

The editor of a regional Christian magazine invited me to write an article on grief. "Not sugarcoating the feelings of grief," he said in his email, "but rather acknowledging and even endorsing the process of grief. A pastoral article, yes, but also the article of one who lives the same journey. One who also anticipates, and lives with, the empty places."

I was still so much in process that I wasn't sure I could write an article on grief, or even if I wanted to. But here was an opportunity to give. Out of the consolation I had received, perhaps it was time to share that consolation with others. As the apostle points out in one of his letters to the Corinthian church, God is "the one who comforts us in all our trouble so that we can comfort other people who are in every kind of trouble. We offer the same comfort that we ourselves received from God" (2 Corinthians 1:4).

Yet how could I take my huge and painful experience, and set it down in words? What encouragement could I offer others who might be grieving? I felt such a poverty of spirit. But out of that poverty, I wrote the article and gave what I could.

Through Grief to Giving

HOPE PRACTICE

If you don't feel ready to give—if just the thought makes you feel guilty or sick or impatient or something else that you can't name—feel free to skip this part. Give yourself the gift of grace.

But if you feel stuck in a pigeonhole of loss and want to break out, perhaps this story of the poor widow can point a way forward for you. She first drew near to God, which might have been expected in her time and culture. But by giving her two coins, she did an unexpected thing. She took a risk, gave her all, and Jesus delighted in her giving.

Whatever your loss, whatever your experience of poverty in thoughts, feelings, spirit, or material things, consider how you might draw near to God. Will you draw near to God by going to a place of worship and bringing an offering? By spending time at home in silence, or listening to music? In Scripture and prayer? Walking outdoors in God's creation? Or in some other way?

Consider what you might give. Money? Time? Attention? And to whom or what? Even in times of need, even as we grieve, at some point in our journey, perhaps we too can take our eyes off ourselves, look to God, and express our grief in giving. Then may we receive God's comfort and joy.

26

A CHANGING LANDSCAPE

Grief is like a long valley, a winding valley where any bend may reveal a totally new landscape.
  C.S. LEWIS, *A Grief Observed*

Eighteen months after my Dearheart died, someone asked me, "How did you deal with your grief?"

How *did* you deal with your grief? My mind immediately translated the question into the present tense: "How *are* you dealing with your grief?" I might have looked all together on the outside, but on the inside I was still healing, and in this life, perhaps I always will be. The grief that descended when my Dearheart died remains with me, keenly felt in small, everyday ways, and as I now make larger decisions without him by my side as before. Yet even as grief continues, I sense a difference in my grieving.

Since Elisabeth Kubler-Ross's work on the five stages of grief, others have posited three stages, seven, or some other number.

Hope Beyond Our Sorrows

Psychologists Margaret Stroebe and Henk Schut working in the Netherlands have taken a functional approach with their dual process model.[1] They envision the tasks of grieving as either *loss-oriented* or *restoration-oriented*. Loss-oriented tasks are those we might generally think of as grief work: getting used to loss and learning to let go. Restoration-oriented tasks include trying new things, taking on new roles and relationships, and distracting oneself to provide respite from grief. Stroebe and Schut note that people dealing with loss tend to go between these two types of tasks while also attending to the tasks of daily life. Over time, as they process their grief and become more engaged in everyday living, the challenges of loss and restoration tend to recede.

I haven't tried to fit my experience into any one particular model of grief, but my own view of early, middle, and present grief seems to track well with the dual process. In my early grief when I felt stuck in molasses, I went back and forth between what Stroebe and Schut identify as loss-oriented work and restoration-oriented work. I took time to mourn my loss, but at times I would distract myself from grief by binge-watching *Law and Order* and other DVDs from my Dearheart's collection—television shows instead of movies, plots and problems that resolved in an hour instead of more difficult, ongoing situations that were too much like real life.

In my middle grief as I started to get unstuck, I began writing again and engaging more in daily life. But I continued with loss-oriented tasks like completing my Dearheart's final tax return, and restoration-oriented tasks like learning to do some of the household chores that he used to do and taking on a new role as editor of *Rejoice!* devotional magazine.

A Changing Landscape

In my present grief, daily life seems even more back to normal, with less time overall taken up with loss-oriented and restoration-oriented tasks, although some still remain like traces of molasses. Just this past week, I finally arranged for the electric bill to be transferred to my name. "We can't bill a deceased person," said the voice on the phone, although the company had been doing just that for over two years since my Dearheart's death.

"I realize I should have called earlier," I said, "but the bills arrived digitally as usual, and I had always been the one to pay them, so I simply continued. I'm sorry it's taken me this long, and I appreciate your help in making the change." That was another loss-oriented task in the midst of daily life—one more piece of the chaos of grief that's now been settled—yet I know that there are still a few more hangers-on that I will need to address.

This has been my changing landscape of grief, with a new landscape around each bend as C. S. Lewis describes. But the landscape of grief is different for each of us. Our losses are different. Our personalities and backgrounds are different. We may be on a similar journey of grief, but each of our journeys is unique.

Naomi and her two daughters-in-law, Ruth and Orpah, had all been married, but one by one, their husbands died until all three of the women were left as widows. Three women. Three griefs. Three different paths of healing. For Naomi, the path forward meant returning to Judah where she was born. Ruth accompanied her, but for Ruth, the trip was not a homecoming, but a move to a foreign country. Orpah also started out for Judah with Naomi and Ruth, and the three women supported one another along the way.

But then Naomi urged both of her daughters-in-law to return to their parents' homes in Moab. Why should they uproot their lives and start over in Judah? Moab was at least home to them, and they could perhaps more easily start new lives there. Orpah agreed, while Ruth continued with Naomi. In the book of Ruth, Orpah's story ends with Orpah kissing her mother-in-law goodbye (Ruth 1:14). We have no idea whether Orpah made her way safely home, whether her parents welcomed her back, whether she remarried and started a new family. Though all three were widows, Naomi, Ruth, and Orpah each had a distinctly different journey.

It's often recommended not to make any major life decisions for at least six months after the death of a spouse or other traumatic event. Grief can make it difficult to think clearly and can cloud your judgment, so it's best to wait. But depending on your particular journey, that may or may not be the best advice. After the death of her sister, when Amanda Held Opelt began to question her faith, she wisely decided not to decide. She writes, "I decided to wait, to watch, to pray. I decided to be patient, to not come to any conclusions, at least not right away."[2]

Soon after Ann Brenoff's husband died, she made two major decisions: to quit her job and put their home up for sale.[3] During the two years of caring for her sick husband, she had already done much of her grieving, so she and their

A Changing Landscape

children felt more than ready for these changes. When his wife and daughter died, one man couldn't face living at home without them, so he moved to a small apartment by himself. For some people, financial or other reasons may require a move or other major changes with little lead time. In grief, the landscape keeps changing, and each personal landscape is unique.

A Changing Landscape

HOPE PRACTICE

One Sunday morning, I read these words in the front of our worship folder:

> I will lead the blind by ways they have not known,
>   along unfamiliar paths I will guide them;
> I will turn the darkness into light before them
>   and make the rough places smooth.
> These are the things I will do;
>   I will not forsake them.
> —Isaiah 42:16 (NIV)

I immediately took these as words of comfort in times of loss, disappointment, and broken dreams. God will lead us on this path we don't know. God will give us light and establish our steps. Even when we feel abandoned by others—abandoned by those who have died, abandoned by those who ignore or don't understand our grief—God will never abandon us. Whatever my particular journey of grief, God will never abandon me.

Imagine the landscape of your grief as it is today. How does it look to you? Are you traveling a familiar path or one that is new to you? Is your path rough or relatively smooth? If it's helpful,

A Changing Landscape

you may wish to take a piece of paper and draw your landscape. In the first few weeks after my Dearheart's death, I might have taken a dark brown crayon and filled a page with it to express the heaviness I felt. Lighter now, I might imagine my piece of paper like the sky and draw a bit of sun. If you're more of an artist, you might draw a peaceful scene or do something more abstract to express your emotions, whatever your landscape looks like for you today.

Then take a step back and survey your journey. Wherever it has taken you, God has been with you. Wherever you are at this point, Jesus walks with you. Wherever you go, God's Spirit surrounds you and will never forsake you.

27

MORE COMPLICATED GRIEF

Grief isn't something you only do once.
EDITH EGER, *The Gift*

As a nonexpert, I'd say that all grief is complicated. People are complicated—with different personalities, different family relationships or no relationship, different cultural and ethnic backgrounds, different religious and nonreligious beliefs and practices. I could go on listing different personal and social dynamics, but you get my meaning—people are complicated, which makes grief complicated too.

But when professionals speak of complicated grief, they generally mean a more prolonged and intense experience of grieving. Complicated grief—sometimes referred to as chronic grief or a prolonged grief disorder—may look like depression or anxiety. It may be related to specific trauma. Complicated grief interferes with everyday life—making it difficult to plan or follow through with family, work, or other responsibilities. That kind of confusion and disruption can be part of any grief, but with more complicated grief, the sense of disbelief and inability to adjust may go on and on, perhaps for a year or more.

Hope Beyond Our Sorrows

In 1655, Hannah Allen was seventeen years old and newly married. Over the next few years, her merchant husband was often away at sea, and she would suffer from bouts of depression. In her mid-twenties, her husband died while on one of his travels, leaving Hannah as a single mother to raise their young son, and deepening her depression, now complicated by her sudden grief.

During this time, Hannah struggled with obsessive thoughts, with feelings of despair, and she attempted suicide more than once. Her family and friends stood by her, and did what they could to offer support. She prayed and turned to the church for pastoral care. While the therapies and medications available to us were unknown in her day, she sought out medical treatment, and most of all, she sought for God.

In her reflection on Hannah's story, author Diana Gruver writes:

> The cure for Hannah Allen wasn't to drag her to church. It wasn't to convince her to pray more. It wasn't to quote Scripture at her until it removed her despair. Her caretakers sought for her the best medical care of the day. They changed her surroundings. They put her on what we would now call suicide watch. They kept showing up with compassion. They attended to her soul, yes, but they also attended to her body.
>
> Was God still at work? Absolutely. Hannah tells us herself that God, in his mercy, was still with her in her darkest days. He was still present and working in the pain. But this didn't stop her from seeing a doctor.[1]

More Complicated Grief

When it comes to complicated grief today, we need that same kind of wholistic approach. Yes, prayer and Scripture and turning toward God. Yes, community in the form of family, friends, church, and others. Yes, healthy self-care for body, soul, mind, and spirit. Yes, support groups and counseling and medical care. All of these things may seem overwhelming, and they are. But each one, given their due, played a part in Hannah Allen's time of need. And by God's grace, may each one give us a place to start as we grieve and heal.

In *The Grieving Brain*, Dr. Mary-Frances O'Connor shares the story of Vivian as an example of complicated grief.[2] After forty years of marriage, Vivian's husband died, but Vivian continued to shop and cook for two as she had before. Every night she cooked two meals, ate one, and threw the other away. This went on for months. Vivian couldn't seem to stop herself, yet she found her own behavior so troublesome that she hid it from her family.

Vivian eventually sought therapy for her complicated grief. The therapist guided her in a number of different strategies. Vivian learned more about the grieving process, how to revisit the memory of her husband in the hospital and accept the reality of his death, how to observe and record her own thoughts and feelings. With the help of her therapist, Vivian worked at building new social connections and other personal skills.

Vivian also talked with her therapist about how she continued to prepare two meals and throw one away. But instead of simply telling her to stop, the therapist asked what Vivian could do with the extra food. Over time, Vivian decided to freeze the extra meals, and then when she learned that her church was delivering meals to people in need, she began to donate the meals to their ministry.

With therapy, Vivian learned how to move with her grief in a healthier way. Instead of stopping her long-established pattern of cooking meals for two, she found a way to transform it. Being involved in the church's meal ministry gave her a new sense of purpose, a new outlet, and new healthy connections with other people.

Grief is a natural response to loss, but as we grieve, not every response is a healthy one. If rage makes you violent or abusive to yourself or others, if you feel suicidal, if you have recurring thoughts or patterns of behavior that are troublesome to you—so troublesome that you hide them from others as Vivian did—please follow her example and seek professional help.

You may find it easier to start with a pastor, a grief support group leader, your doctor, or someone else you know, but be aware that they may not be fully equipped to help you. Think of them more as first contacts, as companions on the way who can help point you to the more specific help you need.

More Complicated Grief

HOPE PRACTICE

Dr. Edith Eger is a Holocaust survivor and psychologist who has worked with military veterans and others who have suffered physical and mental trauma. She was sixteen years old when she and her family were sent to Auschwitz, where her parents were both murdered, and she endured the horrors of the concentration camp for eight months until it was liberated in 1945.

In *The Choice: Embrace the Possible*, she tells her story of resilience and healing from the trauma she experienced. In *The Gift: 12 Lessons to Save Your Life*, she shares some of the practices that have helped her and her patients. "*The Gift* is like a workbook for *The Choice*," said one of my friends who recommended Dr. Eger's work to me.

In her chapter on unresolved grief, Dr. Eger offers this key:

> If someone you love has died, give yourself thirty minutes every day to honor the person and the loss. Take an imaginary key, unlock your heart, and free your grief. Cry, yell, listen to music that reminds you of your loved one, look at pictures, read old letters. Express and be with your grief, 100 percent. When the

Hope Beyond Our Sorrows

thirty minutes have passed, tuck your loved one safely inside your heart and get back to living.[3]

Feel free to take that half an hour now if you need it. Then return to your daily life.

28

NO MORE DEATH,
NO MORE GRIEVING

*Death will be no more. There will be no mourning,
crying, or pain anymore, for the former things have
passed away.*
REVELATION 21:4

A year and some months after my Dearheart's death, a
friend invited me to an evening of classical music. She
had started a small ensemble with several other professional
musicians: herself and another soprano who also plays cello, a
flautist, violinist, and pianist. Along with another friend who
would be running the sound and livestream for the group, they
called themselves Augmented Five. *Nuit Enchantée* was their
debut concert, featuring mainly French, Russian, and Italian
music arranged for solos, duets, trios, and quintets.

I am not well versed in classical music, so I expected that
most of the program would be new to me, and I was right.
I recognized the names of Debussy and Rimsky-Korsakov,
but didn't know the pieces listed with their names. I'd never
heard of Chaminade or Caplet or Massanet. But what a treat!
I delighted in the richness of the music and read the words
of translation thoughtfully provided on the screen above
the musicians.

195

It was all wonderful, but by the end of the evening, I also felt terribly sad. There were so many love songs—the nightingale serenading the rose, the dawn shining with love, the longing for a lost love. I longed for my lost love too. Then I read the English translation of Jules Massanet's Élégie to close the program, the very last words: "all is withered for evermore!"

I joined everyone in applause for such a stirring evening of music and words. My heart and mind and soul were full. But inwardly, I protested. What? We're ending with everything frozen and withered? Withered for evermore? How could such a glorious evening end on such a note of despair?

Thankfully, the concert didn't end that way. The group continued with an encore: "Barcarolle" from Jacques Offenbach's opera *Les Contes d'Hoffman* (The Tales of Hoffman). *Belle nuit, ô nuit d'amour.* I could rely on my high school French for the translation: "Beautiful night, O night of love." And then *Ah! souris à nos ivresses!* I had to look up that line: "Ah! Smile upon our joys!"

Like a biblical lament moving from the soul's anguish to affirmation of faith and praise for God's goodness, the evening had given voice to longing and great sorrow, but did not stop there. With the final piece, the tears dissolved into a smile, and despair gave way to joy. Love had not withered to nothing for evermore. Joy had returned at last!

With Jesus' death, his life and ministry had come to a brutal end. He would no longer travel the countryside with his disciples. No longer preach to crowds in the open air, or teach in

No More Death, No More Grieving

the synagogue. No longer walk on water or perform miraculous healings. All of that was done and gone.

And what of Jesus' promises of new life and lasting peace? He had fallen like a grain of wheat, crushed by those who opposed him, and executed on a cross by the authorities. His disciples had scattered. In fear and confusion, some withdrew to a locked room. Some left Jerusalem to return home. They had many questions—and no peace. Much heartache—and no relief. Love in the person of Jesus had left them, gone for evermore.

Or so they thought. But that was not the end of the story. Three days later, new life unfolded, and God raised Jesus from the dead! The risen Christ appeared to Mary in the garden (John 20:11–17). He met two of the disciples on the road to Emmaus (Luke 24:13–35). He came to the other disciples in their locked room and spoke peace to them (John 20:19–29). He met the disciples again at the sea of Tiberias where some of them had gone fishing. He even served them bread and fish for breakfast (John 21:1–14). The disciples could hardly believe that Jesus had returned to them. Joy had returned at last!

When God raised Jesus to new life, the sting of death was reversed.

As the apostle Paul writes:

Death has been swallowed up by a victory.
Where is your victory, Death?
Where is your sting, Death?
—1 Corinthians 15:54–55

Hope Beyond Our Sorrows

In this life we know the sting of death: in the absence of a loved one, in the anxiety of a life-threatening diagnosis, in the restless nights of tossing and turning that can come with any broken dream. The sting of death is the pain of loss. The sting of death is the loneliness that can't be relieved no matter how much we pray, no matter how many other people may surround us, no matter how many phone calls or emails or cards. In this life, death might well look like defeat.

But the sting of death—although painful and real—is limited. The sting of death is part of this time-bound, perishable world. From the view of eternity, it's really death that has been defeated. For while we may speak of death as a final goodbye on this earth—from the view of eternity, that goodbye is not final. Death has lost its sting. Its power has been taken away—for God raised Jesus to new life, delivers us from the power of sin and death, and grants us new life here, now, and into eternity.

That's the testimony of the apostle Paul in his letter to the Corinthian church: "Thanks be to God, who gives us this victory through our Lord Jesus Christ!" (1 Corinthians 15:57). For the Corinthian church centuries ago, and for us today, this victory over death is more than a theological statement, more than a theory or an intellectual belief or a philosophy. It makes a difference to the way we live, for immediately following this expression of thanks and victory, the apostle continues:

> As a result of all this, my loved brothers and sisters, you must stand firm, unshakable, excelling in the work of the Lord as always, because you know that your labor isn't going to be for nothing in the Lord.
> —1 Corinthians 15:58

No More Death, No More Grieving

For all the sting of death in this life, one day death will be no more. One day the perishable will give way to the imperishable. So even as we grieve, we do not grieve as those who have no hope (1 Thessalonians 4:13). Death may shake us. Grief may make us quiver. Yet we stand on the unshakeable good news of victory. We have this hope beyond our sorrows. Even in the face of grief and death, God will comfort and steady us. We can move beyond despair to go on living, to go on following Jesus, to go on doing the work that God has placed before us. This life is not in vain, for there is more to come.

No More Death, No More Grieving

HOPE PRACTICE

First Corinthians 15 reminds us that this life is not all there is. Even the most blessed life on this earth is not all there is. The best is yet to come. This beautiful, precious, fragile, perishable, human life will one day give way to the imperishable!

But that's no reason to live idly or carelessly in this life. In the Thessalonian church of the New Testament, some had simply stopped working, perhaps because they believed the end was near. If Jesus was coming again, why bother working? So some set down their tools and refused to work. With too much time on their hands, they made trouble for other people, and relied on others who had to work twice as hard to support them (2 Thessalonians 3:11).

Today, some may use the same misguided logic. If this world is only temporary, why bother taking care of it? If the best is yet to come, why work at making this world a better place? Why bother working at all? But to the Thessalonian church and for us today, there remains this clear instruction:

No More Death, No More Grieving

By the Lord Jesus Christ, we command and encourage such people to work quietly and put their own food on the table.
—2 Thessalonians 3:12

Consider what work God has set before you today. It may be as mundane as setting out your recyclables for pick up, or getting the children off to school, or getting supper on the table. It may or may not be related to housework or paid employment or volunteer work for your church or community. It could be the work of prayer, or hospitality, or saying a kind word to someone who needs it. Whatever work God has placed before you, do it now and do it quietly without calling attention to yourself. Do it well, "excelling in the work of the Lord" (1 Corinthians 15:58). For one day, there will be no more death and no more grieving.

29

GOD RESTORES ALL THINGS

The key to facing major loss is holding on to Jesus'
promise of resurrection: in the end, we will get back what
we lose in death.

CURTIS CHANG, *The Anxiety Opportunity*

After my Dearheart died, the women of my writers guild sent me a lovely care package that included a copy of *Picturing Heaven: 40 Hope-Filled Devotions with Coloring Pages* by Randy Alcorn. Each devotion is a single page, reflecting on God's promise to make all things new. Then on the facing page is a drawing for coloring, and as part of their care package, my writer friends thoughtfully included a set of dual-tip brush pens in thirty-six beautiful colors.

In his meditation on heaven, Alcorn writes:

> Our pain and suffering may or may not be relieved in this life, but they will certainly be relieved in the life to come. That is Christ's promise—no more pain or death! He will wipe away all our tears. Jesus took on our sorrows so that one day we would be free from them all.[1]

Across from these words, on the facing page of the book, is one of the drawings meant for coloring. It features the face of a woman who is weeping—with the hand of God catching her tears and releasing them to water a beautiful garden of flowers at the bottom of the page. Heaven will mean no more tears, the earth restored like a garden, and all life will be made new!

In the Bible, the word *heaven* is used in a number of different ways. In some places, heaven is simply the sky above us. So Psalm 78:23 says, "God gave orders to the skies above, opened heaven's doors." In other places, heaven is God's "holy home" (Deuteronomy 26:15). Our God is "the God of heaven" (Ezra 1:2). Sometimes the word heaven is used as a reverent way of referring to God, as in the gospel of Matthew which often says the kingdom of heaven in place of the kingdom of God. In the Lord's Prayer, heaven is the place that fully expresses the will of God: "Bring in your kingdom so that your will is done on earth as it's done in heaven" (Matthew 6:10). In God's new heaven to come, there will be no more dying, no more sorrow, no more pain (Isaiah 65:17–25; Revelation 21:1–5).

Will heaven really have pearly gates, streets of gold, and many mansions? Who can say? The Bible's poetic imagery stretches the limits of human language and imagination. It's just not possible to describe how wondrous, how glorious heaven will be.

But the prophet Isaiah tries. After the announcement of God's intention—"Look! I'm creating a new heaven and a new earth" (Isaiah 65:17)—the rest of the chapter is commentary. God's new heaven and earth will be a place of rejoicing

God Restores All Things

and delight (vv. 18–19), a place of life instead of death (v. 20), where people will build houses and never be forced out of them, where they will plant vineyards that will not be taken away from them (vv. 21–23). The people will have such close communion with God that they will receive an answer even before they call (v. 24). All creation and even animals that might be natural enemies will live in harmony with one another (v. 25).

Isaiah's message of hope came to a people in deep grief. After many attacks and many years of labor, they had rebuilt the temple as a place of worship, but it was much less glorious than the original temple. The city walls were still in ruins. Where there used to be houses and busy public markets, there was still rubble. The people experienced many conflicts over what to do and how best to move forward. They faced idolatry and other spiritual challenges. They were surrounded by the same old ruins and the same old work and the same old tensions.

Into that setting of grief and brokenness came God's word of hope: "Be glad and rejoice forever in what I'm creating" (Isaiah 65:18). This vision is echoed in 2 Peter 3:13: "according to his promise we are waiting for a new heaven and a new earth, where righteousness is at home." And again in Revelation 21:1: "Then I saw a new heaven and a new earth."

This vision is not simply pie in the sky for some distant future. God is creating a new heaven and a new earth even now. So we can pray even now, knowing that God hears us before we call. We can have compassion for others even now, because one day there will be no more suffering or sorrow or pain. We can be glad and rejoice—not only in that day to come, but even now. Because for all of us, forever starts today.

That goes for all of us who are grieving too. One day there will be a new heaven and a new earth where grief and sorrow are no more. God will wipe away our tears, lay all our anxieties to rest, and we will be at peace. So in keeping with that vision, let us build and plant and do good works today and forever. Let us live into God's peace and live fully today and forever. Let us call on God and be glad and rejoice today and forever.

"I think you'll enjoy this podcast with Curtis Chang," a friend said to me. "Some of what he says reminds me of the themes in your writing." And yes! I loved the podcast, and Curtis Chang's book was even better.

In his book *The Anxiety Opportunity: How Worry is the Doorway to Your Best Self*, Chang shares some of his own experience with anxiety, pastoral burnout, and recovery. He anchors his discussion of anxiety in the losses we experience in this life, and sets all of that in a broader context of Western history and philosophy. He gives a quick review of three main ways of coping with loss in the ancient world and today. The Stoics would say, "Do good despite loss." The Epicureans: "Enjoy life despite loss." Platonism: "Your loss is not real."[2]

In contrast, Chang lifts up the Christian view of loss:

We get back what we lose—and more.

The "and more" comes in because Christian resurrection gives back eternal bodies. Our bodies will be raised in imperishable form (1 Corinthians 15:42–57). We are saved from all future loss as well. We get back what we lose and will get to keep it all because death itself will finally be defeated forever.[3]

God Restores All Things

God will restore all things! (Acts 3:21). That makes a difference to how we bear loss and anxiety in this life. That makes a difference to how we grieve. That makes a difference to how we enjoy life, do good in this world, and engage in acts of restoration even now as signposts of the fullness of God's restoration to come.

God Restores All Things

HOPE PRACTICE

Stand with your arms outstretched on either side of you. Close your eyes and imagine God showering you with all the things you have lost in this life. Your lost confidence—restored. Your lost identity and sense of safety—restored. Our lost loved ones—do we dare believe that one day they will be restored to us too? I know some imagine being welcomed into heaven by a dearly departed spouse, by parents who have passed on years before, by a whole company of saints. While Scripture speaks clearly of the resurrection of the body and the restoration of all things, we're not given specific details about what that might look like. In this as in many other matters, we walk by faith, not by sight.

So let us accept the mystery of what we don't know. And let us embrace God's promise to restore all things. Bring your arms in and give yourself a hug. In Jesus Christ, God is making all things new.

30

GOD COMES TO US

*God is with us. God does hold us, even when we don't
know it. Even when we can't hold on to God, God holds
on to us.*

AUNDI KOLBER, *Strong Like Water*

Last summer, I received an invitation to my former church where I had served as a pastor. Terry was getting baptized, and I was invited to participate in the worship service. What a delight! I had known Terry for many years, and we had talked about faith, church, and baptism. He had lived out his faith in many ways—he and his wife had raised their children in the church, he had been part of a small group, and a consistent volunteer running the sound system for worship—but he had never taken the formal step of baptism. Now the time had come!

It was such a privilege to be invited for the celebration, and I wanted to be there, of course. But it would be my first time at the church for a worship service since I had resigned as pastor over five years ago. After twenty-five years of congregational ministry, the time had come to focus more on my writing and ministry beyond the local church. I had needed to let go and follow the Spirit's leading to reorient

Hope Beyond Our Sorrows

my ministry in a new direction. The church had needed to let go to form a new relationship with a new pastor. So I hadn't returned for Sunday worship since my farewell service, and the church hadn't invited me. Until now. My first time at Sunday worship since I had resigned. My first time—without my Dearheart—worshiping in the church that had been home to both of us.

The worship leader told me that the empty pitcher for baptism would be at the front of the church, and asked if I could bring some water to add to it while the congregation sang "As I Went Down to the River to Pray." "You can bring it in whatever container you feel appropriate," she said. About ten people who had played a significant role in Terry's life were being asked to bring water, and the children would also add some water as part of their story time. Just that detail made me homesick for my former church. I had loved the creativity in worship while I had served there, and that at least hadn't changed.

I chose to bring the water in a tiny red jar with a beautiful, gold lid that had belonged to my mother. Although she and my dad were married in the United Church, they hadn't baptized me or any of my sisters as infants. I once asked her why, and she said, "We thought you should make your own decision." That's exactly what Terry had done—he hadn't been baptized as a teenager like some of his peers, but had made his own decision at his own pace. I later learned that Terry's brother had brought water from the family home where they had grown up. A close friend had brought water from a stream where they would go hiking. Such thoughtful, beautiful responses deepened my appreciation for the day and heightened my already high emotions.

God Comes to Us

I was greeted warmly in the parking lot and in the foyer as I made my way to the sanctuary. It was a lovely reunion with so many familiar and dearly loved people. When I went forward to add my water to the pitcher, I paused to pray for Terry and for the congregation. I paused to feel the weight of the moment—the joy of celebration for Terry and the church, and the sweet, sad nostalgia of coming home. For in that moment, I felt at home, yet not home. Still part of the family, yet perhaps more like a distant relative, especially without my Dearheart.

In the communion service that followed the baptism, the worship leader invited us to come to the table. "Come," she said. "Jesus himself will serve us. Come."

I watched for an usher to direct us forward from the pews. But no usher appeared. No one got up. Instead, all of us remained seated where we were. Only the deacons went forward, then came to the congregation with their baskets of bread. Each deacon wore gloves—perhaps a practice that started during the coronavirus pandemic. Each took a piece of bread and placed it in each outstretched hand. Piece by piece. Hand to hand. It was the same with the cup. We all remained seated, and the deacons came with their trays of tiny cups, and served each person. Cup by cup. Hand to hand.

My first thought was how curious that seemed. While we had been invited to come, we all remained seated. And invitation notwithstanding, the communion service had been planned for the deacons to come to us. Our only response was simply to receive. That's when I had my *aha* moment—instead of our coming to the table, the deacons had brought God's table to us.

That's how it is in life—God's invitation is ever before us. Come and taste. Come and drink. Come and rest. Come join the party!

> All of you who are thirsty, come to the water!
> Whoever has no money, come, buy food and eat!
> Without money, at no cost, buy wine and milk!
> —Isaiah 55:1

> Come to me, all you who are struggling hard and carrying heavy loads, and I will give you rest.
> —Matthew 11:28

> The Spirit and the bride say, "Come!" Let the one who hears say, "Come!" And let the one who is thirsty come! Let the one who wishes receive life-giving water as a gift.
> —Revelation 22:17

We are always invited, yet what happens is that God comes to us—always, always, comes to us. The heavens tear open as the psalmist imagines:

> People are like a breath;
> their lives are like passing shadows.
> LORD, tear open the sky and come down.
> —Psalm 144:4–5 (NCV)

God comes to us in the eating and drinking of communion. In our weakness and when we are most vulnerable in grief

God Comes to Us

and trouble, God comes to us. In the tears at a funeral. In the quiet losses and griefs we bear each day. God comes to us in our early, middle, and present grief, wherever we may find ourselves.

Yes, we are invited to come, and joyfully received when we're able to take up God's invitation. But when we feel paralyzed, when we feel too tired or weak or wounded to move, God comes to us. God comes to you even now, in this moment.

God Comes to Us

HOPE PRACTICE

> I will seek out the lost, bring back the strays, bind up the wounded, and strengthen the weak.
> —Ezekiel 34:16

Rest now in God's welcome. Breathe in God's presence: one, two, three, four, five. Breathe out anxiety and fear: one, two, three, four, five, six, seven.

Feel the weight of this moment: the joy and the sorrow for what once was and now is.

Accept the divine invitation to taste and see that God is good. Receive God's peace that passes all understanding. Be assured that God is with you. As Jesus says, "Look, I myself will be with you every day until the end of this present age" (Matthew 28:20). May the Spirit grant you fresh vision and lead you forward.

AFTERWORD

I started writing this book in earnest two years and some months after my Dearheart passed away. By the time this book is published, it will be over three years since his death, and whenever you read this, even more time will have passed. From the witness of others, I know that there is more beyond the early, middle, and present grief that I've shared, and I hope I've continued to grow in that direction—finding my way forward on sometimes unsteady feet, still leaning on God, still grateful for the support of family, friends, church, and wider community. Thank you, dear readers, for being part of that broad circle of support. May you also find the support you need in whatever griefs you carry. May God be with you and bear you up.

Grief and broken dreams are not the end of the story for any of us. God binds up the brokenhearted (Psalm 147:3). God redeems the brokenness of this world (Isaiah 61:1–4) and makes a new creation (2 Corinthians 5:17). We have that hope now and for the future, bound up in the mystery and power of Jesus' life, death, resurrection, and ascension. In Jesus Christ and by the Spirit, God brings new life!

Hope Beyond Our Sorrows

By God's grace, we can learn to live beyond our broken dreams. I'm praying that for you today. I'm praying that for myself. May the God who numbers the stars and names them (Psalm 147:4) look on us with compassion. May God rebuild the broken ruins of our lives (Isaiah 61:1–4). May we dream new dreams, and live into hope beyond our sorrows one day and one moment at a time.

ACKNOWLEDGMENTS

With Gratitude

As much as I have felt overwhelmed by grief, I am also full of gratitude: for my Dearheart and the life we shared together, for the many people named and unnamed who have been part of my journey, for the opportunity to share faith and hope through my writing, for God's presence that has carried me throughout my days, especially during my early, middle, and present grief. Thank you, thank you, thank you!

When I read a book, I generally read everything including any preface and acknowledgments, since I like to know the background of a book, the people behind it, and notice any names that might be familiar to me. But out of respect for those who prefer not to be named, and since it doesn't seem right for me to name some and not others, I have omitted personal names in these acknowledgments. That does not at all diminish my gratitude for your love, support, and willingness to journey with me. You have my deepest thanks.

For my three sisters, my Dearheart's two brothers, and their families—although we don't live in the same city, I'm grateful for the ways we've managed to stay in touch. We always seem to have a lot to say to each other, so let's talk soon!

Hope Beyond Our Sorrows

For Valley CrossWay Church—your warm welcome has meant so much to me and my Dearheart. You prayed us through many challenges and joys, and accepted me as resident author before any of us knew what that could mean. Thank you for dreaming along with me, for your vision and partnership in ministry.

For friends who appear by name in the chapters of this book and the many more unnamed—thank you for being present in my grieving, for listening, for suggesting books, and for sharing life with me. A special thank you to those whose stories of grief appear as part of this book. You are a gift, and I pray God's ongoing comfort and joy for you.

For my sister members of the Redbud Writers Guild— although I haven't met most of you in person, I'm grateful for your caring and prayers. I've learned so much from you about writing, grieving, and holding on to faith.

For the editors and team at Herald Press—for your encouragement and care with this book, and as I connect with some of you in my role as editor of *Rejoice!*, I'm grateful for your expertise and for your patience as this book slowly took shape. I hope that I won't spend quite so long developing my next idea.

For all of my readers—you may recognize parts of my story that I've shared previously on my websites or published with Godspace, Asian American Women on Leadership, *Light* magazine, or in other places. I'm grateful to these groups and more for supporting my writing and to all of you for reading and providing feedback that has helped me to rethink, re-imagine, revise, and grow.

"May grace be with you all" (1 Timothy 6:21).

NOTES

CHAPTER 1

1. Aundi Kolber, *Try Softer: A Fresh Approach to Move Us Out of Anxiety, Stress, and Survival Mode—and into a Life of Connection and Joy* (Tyndale House Publishers, 2020), 88.

CHAPTER 2

1. Soong-Chan Rah, *Prophetic Lament: A Call for Justice in Troubled Times* (InterVarsity Press, 2015), 127.

CHAPTER 4

1. Sylvia Purdie, *Moving On: Grief in Ministry Transitions* (Philip Garside Books, 2022), 118.

CHAPTER 5

1. Henry F. Lyte, "Abide With Me," 1847, in *Hymnal: A Worship Book* (Brethren Press et al., 1992), 653, verses 1, 2, 4.

CHAPTER 8

1. Jerry Sittser, *A Grace Disguised: How the Soul Grows Through Loss* (Zondervan, 2021, rev. ed.), 38.
2. Anne Peterson, *Real Love: Guaranteed to Last* (self-published, 2012), 32.
3. Gary Roe, *Comfort for Grieving Hearts* (Healing Resources Publishing, 2018), 43.

CHAPTER 9

1. Elisabeth Kubler-Ross, *On Death and Dying: What the Dying Have to Teach Doctors, Nurses, Clergy, and Their Own Families* (Scribner, 1969).
2. Elisabeth Kubler-Ross and David Kessler, *On Grief and Grieving: Finding the Meaning of Grief Through the Five Stages of Loss* (Scribner, 2005), 7.
3. Pam Vredevelt, *Letting Go of Disappointments and Painful Losses* (Multnomah, 2001), 69.

CHAPTER 11

1. Charles Wesley, "Christ the Lord is Risen Today," 1739, in *Hymnal: A Worship Book* (Brethren Press et al., 1992), 280, verse 1.

CHAPTER 12

1. Siân Echard, "The Voyage of Saint Brendan," 2024, https://sianechard.ca/web-pages/1285-2/.
2. Catholic Culture, "Catholic Prayer: Prayer of Saint Brendan the Navigator," https://www.catholicculture.org/culture/liturgicalyear/prayers/view.cfm?id=1467.

CHAPTER 13

1. Bob Deits, *Life After Loss: A Practical Guide to Renewing Your Life After Experiencing Major Loss* (Da Capo Lifelong Books, 6th ed., 2017), 97.
2. Miriam Neff, *From One Widow to Another* (Moody Publishers, 2009), online excerpt https://www.widowmight.org/friendships/.
3. Cheryl Berto, "Church Road Kill: Totally Unacceptable and Too Common," https://whenyouworkforthechurch.com/2020/03/01/church-road-kill/.
4. Anne Mackie Morelli, *When Grief Descends: Suffering, Consolation, and the Book of Job* (As You Wish Publishing, 2020), 2.

CHAPTER 16

1. William Barclay, *A Spiritual Autobiography* (William B. Eerdmans Publishing Company, 1975) 46.

CHAPTER 17

1. April Yamasaki, "How to Get Over a Painful Job Termination—Or Can You?," https://whenyouworkforthechurch.com/2016/07/13/how-to-get-over-a-painful-termination-or-can-you/; "Is There a Better Way to Terminate an Employee?," https://whenyouworkforthechurch.com/2016/09/08/is-there-a-better-way-to-terminate-an-employee/; "Losing Your Job Is Worse than Losing Your Spouse," https://whenyouworkforthechurch.com/2017/08/24/losing-your-job-is-worse-than-losing-your-spouse/.

CHAPTER 18

1. Sheryl Sandberg and Adam Grant, *Option B: Facing Adversity, Building Resilience, and Finding Joy* (Alfred A. Knopf, New York, 2017), 65.

CHAPTER 19

1. Helen Keller, *We Bereaved* (Leslie Fullenwider, Inc., 1929), viii.
2. Trish Hunt, *From Stuck to Unstoppable: The Power of Intentional Decision-Making in Life and Leadership* (Amplify Publishing Group, 2023), Ch. 1.
3. Jerry Sittser, *A Grace Disguised: How the Soul Grows Through Loss* (Zondervan, 2021, rev. ed.), 84.
4. Dorina Lazo Gilmore-Young, *Breathing Through Grief: A Devotional Journal for Seasons of Loss* (Ink & Willow, 2023), 87.

Notes

CHAPTER 21

1. Soong-Chan Rah, *Prophetic Lament: A Call for Justice in Troubled Times* (InterVarsity Press, 2015).

CHAPTER 22

1. Mary-Frances O'Connor, *The Grieving Brain: The Surprising Science of How We Learn from Love and Loss* (HarperOne, 2022), 34.
2. I heard Stuart McLean read this story, but it's also available in print: "Love Never Ends" in Stuart McLean, *Vinyl Café Unplugged* (Penguin Canada, 2009).

CHAPTER 23

1. Daniel G. Amen, *Change Your Brain, Change Your Life* (Harmony Books, 2015).

CHAPTER 24

1. C. S. Lewis, *A Grief Observed* (Valde Books), 21.
2. Elisabeth Kubler-Ross and David Kessler, *On Grief and Grieving: Finding the Meaning of Grief Through the Five Stages of Loss* (Scribner, 2005).
3. Barry Hertz interview with William Shatner, "William Shatner Doesn't Need a Legacy," in the Globe and Mail, October 15, 2022, R3.

CHAPTER 26

1. For a discussion of the dual process model, please see Mary-Frances O'Connor, *The Grieving Brain: The Surprising Science of How We Learn from Love and Loss* (HarperOne, 2022), 75–78.
2. Amanda Held Opelt, *A Hole in the World: Finding Hope in Rituals of Grief and Healing* (Worthy Books, 2022), 207–208.
3. Ann Brenoff, "Rewriting the Manual on Being a Widow," January 20, 2020, https://myprivatevista.com/blogs/resources/rewriting-the-manual-on-being-a-widow.

CHAPTER 27

1. Diana Gruver, *Companions in the Darkness: Seven Saints Who Struggled with Depression and Doubt* (InterVarsity Press, 2020), 47.
2. Mary-Frances O'Connor, *The Grieving Brain: The Surprising Science of How We Learn from Love and Loss* (HarperOne, 2022), 98ff.
3. Edith Eger, *The Gift: 12 Lessons to Save Your Life* (Scribner, 2020), 106.

CHAPTER 29

1. Randy Alcorn, *Picturing Heaven: 40 Hope-Filled Devotions with Coloring Pages* (Tyndale House Publishers, 2017), 86.
2. Curtis Chang, *The Anxiety Opportunity: How Worry Is Your Doorway to Your Best Self* (Zondervan, 2023), 142–143.
3. Chang, 144.

THE AUTHOR

April Yamasaki is an author, editor, and ordained minister with over twenty-five years of experience in congregational ministry. Her writing online and in print focuses on living with faith and hope, including her books: *Sacred Pauses*, *Four Gifts*, *On the Way with Jesus*, and *This Ordinary, Extraordinary Life*. She currently serves as resident author with Valley Cross-Way Church, which is a liturgical worship community; edits the daily devotional magazine *Rejoice!*; and often speaks in churches and other settings. She holds a master of Christian studies from Regent College, Vancouver, B.C. April was happily married to her high school sweetheart until his death two years ago from cancer-related complications. Though grieving, she is grateful for a wonderfully supportive family and church community, good work, good friends, and God's mercies new every morning. For more information and free downloadable resources, visit her websites at AprilYamasaki.com and WhenYouWorkForTheChurch.com.